ETHICAL REASONING

Online Materials

Ethical Reasoning has a companion website for **instructors** containing multiple-choice question sets. The question sets are available as Word documents and in a digital format that can be integrated into a variety of Learning Management Systems.

sites.broadviewpress.com/
ethicalreasoning-instructor

Your access code is:
er38225

Students receive complimentary access to a separate website that provides answers to the exercises included in the text.

sites.broadviewpress.com/
ethicalreasoning

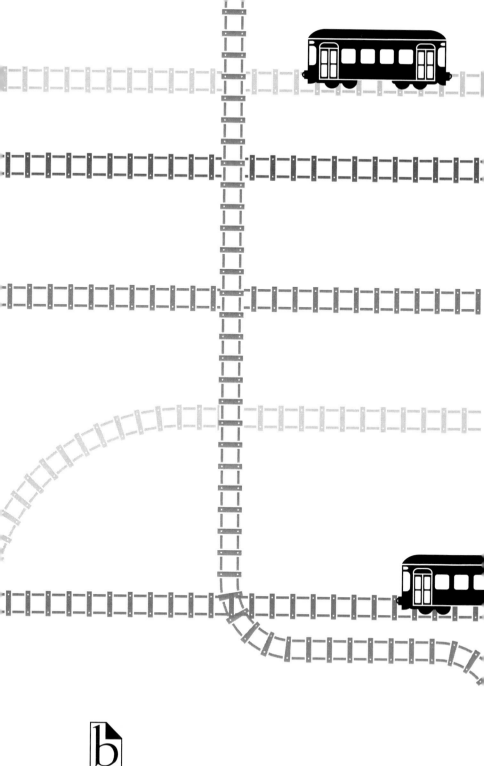

ETHICAL REASONING

THEORY & APPLICATION

ANDREW KERNOHAN

BROADVIEW PRESS — www.broadviewpress.com
Peterborough, Ontario, Canada

Founded in 1985, Broadview Press remains a wholly independent publishing house. Broadview's focus is on academic publishing; our titles are accessible to university and college students as well as scholars and general readers. With 800 titles in print, Broadview has become a leading international publisher in the humanities, with world-wide distribution. Broadview is committed to environmentally responsible publishing and fair business practices.

© 2020 Andrew Kernohan

All rights reserved. No part of this book may be reproduced, kept in an information storage and retrieval system, or transmitted in any form or by any means, electronic or mechanical, including photocopying, recording, or otherwise, except as expressly permitted by the applicable copyright laws or through written permission from the publisher.

Library and Archives Canada Cataloguing in Publication

Title: Ethical reasoning : theory and application / Andrew Kernohan.
Names: Kernohan, Andrew William, 1952– author.
Description: Includes bibliographical references and index.
Identifiers: Canadiana (print) 20200290339 | Canadiana (ebook) 20200290363 | ISBN 9781554814411 (softcover) | ISBN 9781770487611 (PDF) | ISBN 9781460407158 (EPUB)
Subjects: LCSH: Decision making—Moral and ethical aspects. | LCSH: Ethics.
Classification: LCC BJ1419 .K47 2020 | DDC 170—dc23

Broadview Press handles its own distribution in North America:
PO Box 1243, Peterborough, Ontario K9J 7H5, Canada
555 Riverwalk Parkway, Tonawanda, NY 14150, USA
Tel: (705) 743-8990; Fax: (705) 743-8353
email: customerservice@broadviewpress.com

For all territories outside North America, distribution is handled by Eurospan Group.

Canadä

Broadview Press acknowledges the financial support of the Government of Canada for our publishing activities.

Copy edited by Robert M. Martin
Book design by Michel Vrana
Cover images from istockphoto.com

PRINTED IN CANADA

CONTENTS

ACKNOWLEDGMENTS VII
INTRODUCTION IX

CHAPTER 1: THE ROLE OF MORAL THEORY 1
    1.1 Cooperation, Reason, and Emotion   2
    1.2 Universalizability, Reason-Giving, Ought-Implies-Can, and the Is-Ought Gap   9
    1.3 Ethical Relativism   13
    1.4 Ethical Decision-Making   16
    1.5 Identity, Principle, and Consequence   20

CHAPTER 2: BEING A GOOD PERSON 25
    2.1 Virtue Ethics   27
    2.2 Virtue, Cooperation, and Community Membership   30
    2.3 Wisdom and Virtue   33
    2.4 Care Ethics   37
    2.5 Justice and Virtue   41

CHAPTER 3: ACTING ON PRINCIPLE 47
    3.1 Duties 49
    3.2 Moral Rights 53
    3.3 Justifying Moral Rights 56
    3.4 Justice and Moral Equality 59
    3.5 Distributive Justice 61

CHAPTER 4: CREATING GOOD CONSEQUENCES 71
    4.1 Egoism and Contractarianism 74
    4.2 Experience-Based Utilitarianism 78
    4.3 Preference-Satisfaction Utilitarianism 81
    4.4 Economic Utilitarianism 84
    4.5 Indirect Utilitarianism 88
    4.6 Teleological and Holistic Ethics 91

CHAPTER 5: WHO IS RESPONSIBLE? WHO COUNTS? 97
    5.1 Moral Agency 99
    5.2 Causal Responsibility 100
    5.3 Moral Accountability 104
    5.4 Autonomy 106
    5.5 Moral Standing 112

CHAPTER 6: RESOLVING CONFLICT BETWEEN MORAL REASONS 119
    6.1 Ethical Pluralism 120
    6.2 Combining Moral Reasons 124
    6.3 Balancing Moral Reasons 131
    6.4 Fallible Moral Reasoning 135

REFERENCES 143

INDEX 145

ACKNOWLEDGMENTS

Stephen Latta, Philosophy Editor at Broadview Press, proposed this book, read the manuscript, and suggested important revisions to its content and organization.

My colleague, David White, wrote suggested answers to the exercises that appear at the end of each section of the book. His way of putting points is different from mine and will help readers to understand what is, by its nature, an abstract, philosophical text.

Bob Martin edited the content of the final manuscript and saved readers from lots of confusions and mistakes, both glaring and subtle. I take full responsibility for any remaining errors.

Michel Pharand proofread the final manuscript and saved readers from irritating mistakes in spelling, style, and consistency.

An audience at the Dalhousie Philosophy Department Colloquium listened to and commented on an early version of chapter 6, which is now, as a result, much improved.

My partner, Anne MacLellan, lived with me during the lengthy process of authoring this book and still loves me. I dedicate this book to her.

INTRODUCTION

YOU ARE ALREADY, I SINCERELY HOPE, A GOOD PERSON. YOU ARE KIND to your pets, you are honest with your friends, you give money to charity, you do your best to reduce your fossil fuel consumption, and you are indignant when you hear about violations of the rights of other humans and perhaps of animals. If you are not already a good person, then this book is not going to turn you into one. Its aim, instead, is to make you a better person, a person more skilled at making ethical decisions in complicated circumstances.

You learned many of your ethical values as a child, and the rest you internalized, perhaps without a lot of critical reflection, as you grew into an adult. These gut reactions and rules of thumb are adequate for quickly making many of life's decisions. Yet sometimes your ethical situation becomes tricky, and you must reason carefully about what to do. Then, a knowledge of ethical theory is useful.

Since ancient times, philosophers in China, Greece, and India have examined the question of how people should treat one another. Their conclusions went beyond the gut responses that they learned at the knees of their mothers and became general theories about how to be a good person, how to live a principled life, and how to create what is intrinsically valuable. They formulated ethical theories that systematized their conclusions about how people should live together. Ethical theories are neither divine commands nor unbreakable moral laws written into the fabric of the universe. Instead, they are advice, from thinkers who have spent a great deal of time examining such issues, on what are most likely the best ways for people to treat others.

This book offers you a concise grounding in the various concepts and theories behind this ethical advice. Understanding this advice will help you avoid the fallacy of oversimplification. You oversimplify an ethical problem when you look at it thorough the lens of just one ethical perspective. Perhaps you unreflectively follow your gut reaction, or you apply just one ethical maxim, such as the ambiguous utilitarian maxim, "Always act to create the greatest happiness for the greatest number." In contrast, the point of learning about as many ethical theories as possible is that each different theory can draw your attention to a different, but still morally relevant, feature of a problematic ethical situation. The recommendations stemming from these various theories will contribute to your making a more nuanced, better justified, and less simplistic overall decision about what to do.

The problem with this pluralist ethical procedure, and this will be a main theme of the whole book, is that the recommendations stemming from different theories sometimes conflict with one another. For example, when you are considering whether to make a false promise to protect someone else's feelings, the advice to maximize happiness can sometimes conflict with advice to keep promises, or advice to remain the honest sort of person that you are. To resolve such an ethical dilemma, you must balance ethical reasons against one another. You must balance creating happiness against adherence to the principle of promise-keeping and against the damage done to your character by being dishonest. And to do this balancing, you must understand the ethical theories behind why maximizing happiness, promise-keeping, and honesty are morally important.

This book offers you a conceptual toolkit that will help you better integrate ethical considerations into your decisions. It will increase your competence in recognizing ethically problematic situations and in thinking through difficult ethical decisions. It does not offer a decision-making algorithm. It does not offer a code of ethics. It is not a comprehensive discussion of all the ethical issues that may arise. Instead, the book describes a set of ethical approaches that philosophers have formulated over many centuries of reflection. Taken together, these approaches will give you insight into making complex decisions.

Applying abstract ethical theory to specific, ethically problematic, cases is a high-level intellectual task. It is not a skill that you can acquire simply through reading about it. Becoming competent at applying ethical concepts to moral decisions requires not only passively listening to a lecture and reading a textbook, but also actively engaging with difficult cases. Thus, there is another, more pragmatic, reason you should understand and learn the material in this book. If you are reading it, then you are probably enrolled in a university course on moral issues where you are involved in discussing interesting cases and writing about the difficult moral issues involved. You may then regard this book as a sort of checklist of things to consider when writing about one of these cases. You might already know the standard format for a philosophy paper: State your thesis, which in this case will be your decision about what is the best overall course of action. Give reasons for your thesis, where these reasons are drawn from those ethical theories that apply to this case and that support your decision. Consider objections to your thesis, where these objections are drawn from ethical theories that apply to the case but conflict with your decision. Reply to these objections by showing how, in this case, the considerations favoring your decision are stronger than are the objections to it. Repeat the procedure, as required. Doing all this is not a matter of cut-and-paste. To do it well, you need to understand the theories. Never, never, never just quote philosophers such as Aristotle, Bentham, and Kant as authorities about what to do. This is not what philosophy is about. The ethical theories that descend from their writings must stand on their own merits. To apply their advice to a case, you must first understand both its strengths and its weaknesses.

To fully understand the material in this book, I suggest you formulate answers to the questions given at the end of each section of each chapter. Do this before you move on to the next section. The questions are not difficult, and the answers are embedded in the section that you have just read, waiting for you to dig them out. Excavating the answers from the text will help you understand the strengths and weaknesses of the various ethical theories and will help you to remember the important concepts. Answering the questions will also tell you what I consider to be the most important material in the section and could end up giving you a good set of notes on the book. My colleague, David White, has prepared a set of suggested answers to these questions. The answers are available at the publisher's website. Checking your understanding against his answers will be extremely helpful to your understanding. His way of putting things is different from mine, and if you have not fully understood what I have written, then you may understand it better by reading what he has to say.

The book is as concise as I could make it, for which I hope you are grateful. In philosophy, concision comes at the cost of precision, so your instructor will likely point out the places where I am guilty, in my exposition, of the oversimplification I warned you about earlier. I don't feel bad about this; it is all part of the search for understanding. In the last two sections of the concluding chapter, I am guilty of some self-indulgence. I have sketched my own view of the fallible moral reasoning that I have described in the book. Your instructor is welcome to leave these sections off your syllabus, or to take philosophical pleasure in showing how my view is wrong-headed and in offering a better one. Nevertheless, my hope is that you will still end up with a good understanding of ethical reasoning and an appreciation of its usefulness in your life.

> Suggested solutions to the questions in this book can be found at sites.broadviewpress.com/ethicalreasoning/

CHAPTER 1

THE ROLE OF MORAL THEORY

WHENEVER WE CONSIDER WHAT WE OUGHT TO DO, WHAT WE SHOULD do, what it is our duty to do, whether we would be a bad person if we did something, whether something is right or wrong, or whether the results of a decision will be fair to all concerned, then we are making an ethical decision. Most of us live good enough lives without ever really thinking about how we treat others. Moral decisions are often not very difficult. Yet some important decisions about how to live require a great deal of thought.

Ethical decision-making signals itself by the presence of code words such as "ought," "should," "good," "duty," or "fair." The words, "ought," "should," and "good," however, are also used in a non-moral sense. Sometimes what appears to be ethical vocabulary is a prediction, as in, "The meteorologist says that it should rain tomorrow." Sometimes what appears to be ethical vocabulary is a rule of inferences, as in, "From the fact that A is larger than B and B is larger than C, you ought to infer that A is larger than C." Sometimes what appears to be ethical vocabulary is advice about game strategy, as in "In chess, it is wrong to get your queen out early," or "Moving your pawn is a good play." Sometimes it occurs in other sorts of "strategic" advice, as in "To arrive by 9 am, you should catch the 7:30 train." The moral and non-moral uses of this vocabulary are determined by the context. Each of us must, at times, examine our decisions about how to live, and it is this ethical vocabulary that we use in our decision-making.

Human beings are a cooperative species. Without their exceptional ability to work together, humans would still be living in small family groups gathering plants and hunting animals. Ethical principles attempt to systematise a set of recommendations about how moral agents should treat one another and the world around them so that they can successfully cooperate. In this respect, moral systems resemble the legal systems which human beings have created to enable social cooperation. One major difference is that legal systems depend on government power (courts, judges, police, jails, etc.) to make them work, whereas ethical systems depend on people, first, reasoning their way to fair terms of cooperation and, second, having the psychological make-up that is required to stick to those terms.

Each of us has an intuitive understanding of the psychological force, or moral suasion, of an ethical judgment. We understand what someone is saying when she tells us that we ought not to do such-and-such. Ethical judgments have a normative force that motivates us to obey the rules of social cooperation. We learned to understand this action-guiding force of ethical judgments when we were children. In fact, we have understood the force of ethical judgments a lot longer than we have understood the judgments of mathematics, science, or economics. Whereas scientific statements are purely descriptive, ethical judgments contain both a descriptive and a motivating component. For example, advice against non-cooperative behavior, such as "Stealing from Tommy is wrong," implicitly contains both a description of an action about to be performed on Tommy, and either some sort of imperative, "Don't steal from Tommy!" or an expression of emotion, "How terrible of you to steal from Tommy!"

Ethical judgments thus have a dual aspect. On the one hand, they involve the head and its beliefs and reasons. On the other hand, they involve the heart and its feelings and emotions. It turns out that neither head nor heart, reason nor emotion, is enough, by itself, to bring about optimal social cooperation. To properly examine our ethical lives, we must examine both our rational thinking and our emotional responses.

1.1 COOPERATION, REASON, AND EMOTION

For morality to work in enabling social cooperation, people must have both reasoning abilities and the right sort of emotional capacities. This is demonstrated by the interactions involved in two types of games. These games abstract from regular life to illustrate important structural features of ethical situations. The inadequacy of reasoning alone to produce cooperative moral behavior is demonstrated in a well-known bit of game theory, the Prisoner's Dilemma

Game. It demonstrates how agents who can reason well, but who lack any of the prosocial emotions such as empathy, compassion, guilt, shame, admiration, or trustworthiness, will face a cooperation dilemma. The reasoning is tricky, but an understanding of this game should be in everyone's intellectual toolkit. The fact that human beings do have the right sort of prosocial emotions to enable fair cooperation is demonstrated in another game, the Ultimatum Game.

First let us examine how good reasoning alone cannot always produce mutually advantageous cooperation. Imagine two hunters living in a state of nature back in a time before any moral rules had become established. The two hunters must decide whether to trade or fight over their catch. They are from different clans, and each has no sympathy, compassion, or fellow feeling for members of another clan. Though they treat their own families well, they see members of other clans as being members of an alien species. They have no sense of fair treatment for others outside of their own clan. They are neither trusting nor trustworthy. They are, however, totally rational.

In some situations, they will cooperate well enough. Suppose that Gog has caught a live rabbit. Gog does not like rabbit, but he does like partridge. Gog would get zero satisfaction from eating a rabbit, but he would get 2 units of satisfaction from eating a partridge. Conversely, Magog has caught a live partridge, but he prefers rabbit. Magog would get zero satisfaction from eating a partridge, but he would get 2 units of satisfaction from eating a rabbit. In this situation, both hunters could see that their rational course of action is to cooperate by trading their respective catches. If Gog, for example, simply stole Magog's animal, he would not be any better off food-wise than if he traded. Stealing may result in a fight, or at least, in aggravation. In a positive-sum, win-win game such as this, rationality is enough to create cooperation for mutual advantage.

Unfortunately, there are other situations where good reasoning, by itself, is not enough to produce cooperation for mutual advantage. For example, suppose the two hunters have the different preferences. Gog would get 1 unit of satisfaction from eating a rabbit, but he would get 2 units of satisfaction from eating a partridge, and 3 units from eating both. Magog would get 1 unit of satisfaction from a partridge, 2 from a rabbit, or 3 from having both. They can either cooperate by trading, or they can, one or the other or both, decide not to cooperate, and to hit the other man on the head and steal his animal. But if both of them try this last strategy, nobody gains anything; each goes home to his original unsatisfactory catch. In a situation such as this one, it would be mutually advantageous for both hunters to effect a peaceful trade. However, as we shall see, their reasoning processes will rationally result in neither hunter's gaining anything.

To see better what is likely to happen, we can represent their strategic choices in a payoff matrix, as shown in Figure 1.1. A **payoff matrix** for a game is a table that shows each player's payoff for every possible combination of strategies. In this case, the game has two players, Magog and Gog, who each have a choice of two strategies, either to cooperate and try to trade with the other player, or to defect and hit the other player on the head and steal his animal. We represent Magog's two strategies as the two rows of the table, and Gog's two strategies as the two columns of the table. This gives four possible outcomes that we represent by the four cells of the table. Each of these cells shows the payoffs to Magog and Gog of a specific combination of strategies. We show Magog on the left side of the payoff matrix, so we show Magog's payoffs in the lower left of each cell. We show Gog on the upper side of the payoff matrix, so we show Gog's payoffs in the upper right of each cell. For example, if Magog offers to trade but Gog hits him on the head and steals his animal, then their payoffs are in the upper right cell (UR) of the payoff matrix. Magog will end up with 0 units of satisfaction and Gog will get 3. The payoffs in the matrix correspond to the payoffs given in the verbal description of the situation.

		Gog	
		Trade	Steal
Magog	Trade	UL 2 2	UR ✓3 0
	Steal	LL 0 3✓	LR ✓1 1✓

Figure 1.1: Unregulated choices between trading and stealing.

Let us see how this works. Suppose Magog shows up holding his animal and offers to trade. Then what is relevant is the first row of the table. If Gog also shows up willing to trade, then they both do so, and each ends up with 2 satisfaction units (Cell UL). But if Gog shows up intending to steal, he takes Magog's animal, and now has 3, leaving Magog with 0 (Cell UR).

Suppose instead that Magog shows up intending to steal. Now the second row of the table is relevant. If Gog shows up intending to trade, Magog takes his animal, and now has 3 units, leaving Gog with nothing (Cell LL). But, lastly, if Gog shows up also intending to steal, nobody gets anything, and each goes home to his original 1-satisfaction animal (Cell LR). Now consider Magog's reasoning process.

1. First he thinks to himself, "Suppose Gog's going to show up intending to trade. If I came intending to trade, we'd trade, and I'd wind up (UL) with 2 units; but if I hit-and-stole, I'd get his animal without losing my own; so I'd wind up (LL) with 3 units. So, if Gog's going to show up to trade, then I'm better off hitting and stealing than trying to trade."
2. Then he thinks to himself, "But suppose Gog's going to show up intending to hit-and-steal. If I came intending to trade, I'd lose my animal and wind up (UR) with 0 units, but if I came also intending to hit-and-steal, nothing would change hands, and I'd wind up (LR) with 1. Not good, but better than nothing. So, if Gog's going to show up to hit-and-steal, then I'm better off hitting and stealing than trying to trade."
3. Finally, he thinks to himself, "Gee, no matter what Gog does, I'm better off hitting and stealing."

As far as Magog is concerned, LL is better than UL, so we mark his payoff in LL with a checkmark. Similarly, for Magog, LR is better than UR, so we mark his payoff in LR with a checkmark. Magog will conclude that no matter what Gog does, it is rational for him to try to steal. Magog has a dominant strategy. A **dominant strategy** in game theory is a strategy that yields a higher payoff regardless of the strategy chosen by the other player. Figure 1.1 shows that Magog's strategy of stealing has a check mark beside the payoff no matter whether Gog tries to steal or trade. Stealing is Magog's dominant strategy.

Now let us look at Gog's reasoning. Figure 1.1 shows that, no matter which strategy Magog plays, Gog's payoff (also checked) will be higher if he, Gog, attempts to hit and steal. The situation is symmetric, and the reasoning is the same for both Gog and Magog. Therefore, Gog too has a dominant strategy, with both payoffs checked, which is to attempt to steal. It is rational for Gog to attempt to steal as well.

Yet see what happens. If Magog and Gog both follow their totally rational dominant strategy, then they will end up in cell LR, where each will receive a payoff of 1 unit of satisfaction. Their dilemma is that this outcome is not the one that would maximize their rational self-interest. They would both be better off with the outcome shown in cell UL, where they each get 2 units of satisfaction. They can obtain this outcome if they cooperate and both offer to trade, but, by reason alone, they cannot reach this better outcome. Because of the structure of the situation, individually rational decisions will lead to an outcome that is irrational for both parties.

A game is a **Prisoner's Dilemma Game** when both players have dominant strategies that, when played, result in an outcome with payoffs smaller than if each had played another strategy. It gets this name from a strategy sometimes employed by the police to get two criminal accomplices to inform on one another. Even though Magog and Gog are highly intelligent, they do not have the necessary emotional repertoire to trust one another. Because of this they will be unable to achieve the benefits of cooperation. This situation is a paradigm example of a dilemma of cooperation.

Dilemmas of cooperation, such as the Prisoner's Dilemma, show that everyone will be better off if everyone cooperates. They do not show any specific self-interested person that he must cooperate. Instead, they show that people must have cooperative attitudes towards one another if social interactions are to work for everyone. The structure of these cooperative attitudes is the subject matter of ethics. Not every cooperative attitude is fair. For example, if Gog had the attitude of always submitting to Magog's authority, then Magog would do well, but Gog would suffer, and this would be unjust. There could not be a society that worked for everyone if people were incapable of cooperative prosocial attitudes.

In fact, people are capable of cooperative, prosocial attitudes. Evidence for this claim comes from another economic game, the **Ultimatum Game**. The rules of the Ultimatum Game are as follows: The game has two players and a referee. First, the Referee passes some amount of money, for example $10, to Player 1. Player 1 must then issue an ultimatum to Player 2 by offering Player 2 some amount between $1 and $10. If Player 2 accepts the ultimatum, then Player 2 keeps the offer and Player 1 keeps the balance. However, if Player 2 rejects the ultimatum, then the Referee takes back all the money and both players get nothing. For example, Player 1 might offer $3 to Player 2. If Player 2 accepts the ultimatum, then Player 2 gets to keep $3 and Player 1 gets to keep $7. If Player 2 rejects the offer, then neither player gets anything. The game is played just this one time.

The Ultimatum Game appears trivial, but the results are enlightening. Most people, if they imagine themselves in the role of Player 1, would probably offer $5 or a 50/50 split. Most people, if they imagine themselves in the role of Player 2 would probably reject anything but a roughly 50/50 offer because they would consider a lopsided offer to be unfair. Players mostly offer an approximately even split, and players mostly reject offers less than an approximately even split. Perhaps ultimatum-issuing players feel ashamed to offer less than what seems fair or feel compassion for the other player and want to share with them. Perhaps, ultimatum-receiving players feel indignant at unfair offers and angry enough to punish the other players, even at some cost to themselves, and perhaps ultimatum-issuing players know this. It seems that because human beings experience such prosocial emotions, it is possible for them to act ethically.

Notice that if Player 2 is purely rational, she will accept any offer, because even $1 is better than $0. It will cost Player 2 money to punish Player 1 for his unfairness, and according to reasoned self-interest, it would be irrational for Player 2 to take on the cost of punishing Player 1. If she does take on the cost of punishing Player 1, then it must be that she is motivated by the prosocial emotions of indignation and resentment that underlie her sense of injustice.

Ethical systems are stabilized by the prosocial emotions of the agent, emotions such as compassion, sympathy, shame, guilt, indignation, or disgust. When these emotional responses are internalized as character traits, or stable dispositions to react in certain ways, players can count on one another to behave cooperatively. (It may seem strange to say that an emotion like indignation at uncooperative behavior is a prosocial emotion, since indignation can sometimes lead to antisocial behavior. But its role in implementing an ethical system underlying social cooperation justifies this usage.) The prosocial emotions, however, are not all that there is to morality. In the Ultimatum game, it seems obvious that an equal division is a fair division. But in more complicated situations, such as deciding on the division of income in a modern post-industrial economy, what is fair is much less obvious. People do feel indignation at unjust situations, but which situations are unjust is a challenging task to figure out.

Ethical systems can help make social cooperation work. Ethics is only possible because the psychological make-up of human beings enables them to internalize and obey normative rules. However, the prosocial emotions of human beings do not, by themselves, determine the content of the moral rules that agents use in a scheme of cooperation. After all, people can feel indignation at all sorts of situations, not all of which deserve moral condemnation. Morality thus requires the use of ethical reasoning to determine which actions of others merit an agent's indignation and which actions merit admiration and approval. In sum, ethical principles are required to create social cooperation, adherence to ethical principles is possible because human beings have a suite of prosocial emotions and character traits, and ethical principles are determined by a process of ethical reasoning.

When applying ethical reasoning to a problem of how to cooperate with others, we should pay attention both to the emotional reaction that the situation creates in us and to the sorts of ethical principles that summarize centuries of reasoning regarding situations of this sort. Gut reactions are important and helpful, but they are not all there is to ethical decision-making.

1.1 *Exercises*

1. Formulate a definition for each of the following and repeat the definition aloud to help you remember it: (a) prosocial emotion, (b) payoff matrix, (c) dominant strategy, and (d) Prisoner's Dilemma.
2. The police arrest Mike and Nancy as suspects in a robbery and a murder. The police have enough evidence to convict each of them of the robbery, but not of the murder. However, the police can convict one of them of the murder on the testimony of the other. The police put each suspect in a separate interview cell and make each of them the following offer: If both keep silent, then they will each get 2 years in prison for burglary. If they both betray each other, then they will both get 5 years in prison for robbery and murder. If one betrays the other, but the other keeps silent, then the one who does the betraying will get 1 year in prison for the robbery while the other will get 10 years in prison for robbery and murder.
    a) Set up a payoff matrix to represent Mike's and Nancy's options.
    b) After checking to see that you have the correct payoff matrix, solve it to discover if it is a Prisoner's Dilemma. Remember that if Mike and Nancy are rational, then they will try to minimize their prison time.
3. Invent contexts in which the following function as prosocial emotions: (a) guilt, (b) anger, and (c) admiration.
4. Summarize, in your own words, how the Prisoner's Dilemma Game suggests that reason alone cannot lead to social cooperation in all contexts.
5. In the example in the text, what are the total gains from cooperation? How much more preference satisfaction is available for the two players to distribute among themselves if they cooperate than if they fail to cooperate?

6. Summarize, in your own words, how the results of the Ultimatum Game are evidence that people can use prosocial emotions to achieve social cooperation.

1.2 UNIVERSALIZABILITY, REASON-GIVING, OUGHT-IMPLIES-CAN, AND THE IS-OUGHT GAP

When we talk about ethical considerations giving us reasons to act in socially cooperative ways, the word "reason" is ambiguous. A reason can be a motivation for acting in a certain way, or a reason can be a justification for believing one thing rather than another. Ethical reasons, unlike many other reasons, embrace this ambiguity, and have both properties simultaneously. Ethical reasons are **action-guiding** because they motivate us to act in ways that we think are morally right. They do this by engaging prosocial emotions such as guilt at doing wrong and indignation at injustice. At the same time, ethical reasons are **agreement-seeking** because we offer them as justifications to others for acting in a specific way. They are reasons about which there can be argument and debate. When we offer ethical reasons, our goal is to get others to join with us in seeking the truth about which ethical reasons are important, and about what we all should do. Ethical reasons must be persuasive, not coercive.

Descriptive and scientific reasons are agreement-seeking, but not action-guiding. When someone asserts that the climate is changing because human beings are burning fossil fuels, she is asserting something about which there is some public controversy and political debate. She can justify her claim by pointing to scientific evidence about atmospheric carbon dioxide concentrations and to scientific theories about how the greenhouse effect works. Such scientific evidence alone does not provide her with motivation to act in any way. She can easily believe that burning fossil fuel causes climate change without feeling motivated to buy a bicycle or become an environmental activist. Scientific reasons are motivationally inert; by themselves, they do not engage the ethical motivations that lead to action.

In contrast, people's emotional reactions are action-guiding, but are not always agreement-seeking. For example, if someone says that she feels anxious today, she does not thereby mean others should also feel anxious. The emotions involved in ethical judgments move us to action, but at the same time, we care about the agreement of others. When we say that an action is wrong, we would like others to agree with us, to feel the same way about the action as we do, and to stop doing this ethically wrong action. When we make ethical judgments and give ethical reasons, we intend that these reasons apply not only to our own actions, but also to the actions of others. We want others to agree with this so that they will do the right thing.

Because ethical judgments have action-guiding force and factual or scientific statements do not, we cannot logically derive ethical judgments from scientific judgments. There is a logical gap between statements about how the world is and statements about how the world ought to be. Philosophers refer to this important conclusion as the is-ought gap, the fact/value distinction, and the naturalistic fallacy. The **is-ought gap** means that we cannot derive an ethical conclusion from an argument consisting of purely scientific or factual premises. The is-ought gap entails that any argument in favor of an ethical judgment must contain at least one ethical premise. In other words, at least one of the reasons for an ethical decision must be an ethical reason.

The first philosopher to draw attention to the is-ought gap was the eighteenth-century Scottish philosopher David Hume. He wrote the following passage about the work of other philosophers of his time:

> In every system of morality, which I have hitherto met with, I have always remarked, that the author proceeds for some time in the ordinary way of reasoning, and establishes the being of a God, or makes observations concerning human affairs; when of a sudden I am surprized to find, that instead of the usual copulations of propositions, is, and is not, I meet with no proposition that is not connected with an ought, or an ought not. This change is imperceptible; but is, however, of the last [i.e., the greatest] consequence. For as this ought, or ought not, expresses some new relation or affirmation, it is necessary that it should be observed and explained; and at the same time that a reason should be given, for what seems altogether inconceivable, how this new relation can be a deduction from others, which are entirely different from it. But as authors do not commonly use this precaution, I shall presume to recommend it to the readers; and am persuaded, that this small attention would subvert all the vulgar systems of morality ... (Hume 1740: Book III, Part I, Sect. I)

Hume points out the fallacy of reasoning directly from scientific facts to ethical judgments. His advice will lead us to chop off the ethical conclusion of an argument from its purely factual premises. Hence, philosophers sometimes refer to the is-ought gap as Hume's Guillotine.

A second important implication of the action-guiding nature of ethical judgments is that we are not ethically required to do an action if we are unable to perform it. Ethical judgments guide us to perform certain actions, and if we physically cannot perform any of those actions, then we are not obliged to do them. It is a necessary condition of being ethically obliged to perform an action that we can perform that action. For example, we are not ethically obliged to bring about world peace all by ourselves because it is not something that any one person is able to do. The metaethical, **ought-implies-can principle** means that a person cannot be morally obligated to bring about a consequence if he or she is unable to do so. Even to save the world, we cannot be ethically obligated to walk across water or to fly unaided over a mountain.

To put the point less dramatically, ethical obligations may be demanding, but not too demanding. The judgment that we should do everything we can to eradicate world poverty implies that we should give money to effective charities. It does not imply that we should give everything we own to charity and thereby make ourselves destitute and as badly off as the people who we are trying to help. The latter implication is too demanding; it is not something that any of us is able to do.

The ought-implies-can principle is important when we think about holding people morally accountable for their decisions. For example, if someone acts under the threat of physical violence, then we may say she cannot do otherwise. If she cannot do otherwise, then we should excuse her from moral accountability for what she did and blame those who threatened her instead. We must be careful, however, when we apply the ought-implies-can principle. Just because something is an inconvenience does not mean that it is too demanding. If one of us were able to eradicate world poverty by getting up from in front of the television and pressing a button on the wall, then we would not think it too demanding to say that he or she was obliged to do so.

The is-ought gap and the ought-implies-can principle come from the action-guiding, emotional aspect of ethical judgments. Another important constraint on ethical judgments, one that comes from the agreement-seeking aspect of ethical judgments, is that what is right (or wrong) for one person is also right (or wrong) for everyone else. Ethical judgments are **universalizable** because they apply to all moral agents who are similarly situated. Ethical principles only apply to one person but not another if there is some morally relevant difference between the two people. The universalizability of ethical judgments follows from the agreement-seeking property of ethical judgments. Suppose Sally and Ron are both friends of Tina. Sally tells

Ron that he ought to help Tina with her move. At a minimum Sally cannot expect Ron's agreement to this ethical obligation unless she is prepared to admit that she, Sally, also has an obligation to help Tina move. Anything else would be hypocritical. To make a case that Ron has the obligation, but she does not, Sally would need to point to some morally relevant difference between her and Ron. For example, if she is out of town, she could say that she is unable to be there to help with the move, and that there is a morally relevant difference between her and Ron in this situation because of the ought-implies-can principle.

The agreement-seeking aspect of ethical reasoning has another implication. When we are debating with others about what we should do, we must always stand ready to offer other people adequate justifications or good reasons for our claims. The social **practice of reason-giving** consists in always looking for adequate justifications or explanations of our judgments. To give an adequate or good enough reason, such justifications must be morally relevant and not morally arbitrary. In the example above, Sally must meet the requirements of the practice of reason-giving by pointing to a morally relevant reason why she need not help with Tina's move, such as the fact that she is out of town. Merely saying that she is Sally, and that Ron is not, would be an inadequate reason for claiming that she and he have different obligations. The practice of reason-giving also has important consequences when we are thinking about to whom or to what we owe ethical consideration. Why is it ethically permissible to kick rocks but not to kick other human beings? An adequate reason might be that humans can suffer pain and rocks cannot. Is it ethically permissible to kick dogs, but not to kick humans? Do we have a good reason for kicking one but not the other? If the capacity to suffer pain is a morally relevant reason, and if dogs can suffer pain, then we do not have sufficient reason to treat dogs and humans differently. The practice of reason-giving implies that we should not treat cases differently for morally arbitrary reasons.

When applying ethical reasoning to a problem in life, we should remember the following. First, we are not going to solve the problem simply by looking at the facts of the case; we also need to think about the ethical principles on which we are implicitly or explicitly relying. Second, no one can be obliged to do an action that is impossible or even too demanding, though we must be careful to distinguish what is too demanding from what is merely inconvenient. Third, we must consider our own obligations as well as the obligations of everyone else involved. Fourth, we should treat like cases in like ways unless we have good and morally relevant reasons for treating the cases differently.

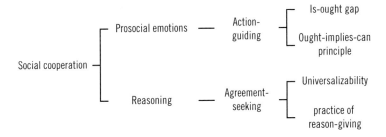

Figure 1.2: Summary of the connections between the ethics of social cooperation and some important metaethical principles.

1.2 Exercises

1. Formulate a definition for each of the following and repeat the definition aloud to help you remember it: (a) Action-guiding feature of moral judgment, (b) agreement-seeking feature of moral judgment, (c) the is-ought gap, (d) the ought-implies-can principle, (e) the universalizability of moral judgments, and (f) the practice of reason-giving.
2. Give an example, different from the ones in the text, of each of the following: (a) someone illegitimately crossing the is-ought gap, (b) a suggested moral requirement that violates the ought-implies-can principle, (c) a suggested moral principle that violates universalizability, and (d) an attempted moral distinction that lacks a sufficient reason.
3. Summarize, in your own words, how the action-guiding feature of moral judgments arises from their emotional aspect.
4. Summarize, in your own words, how the agreement-seeking feature of moral judgments arises from their rational aspect.

1.3 ETHICAL RELATIVISM

Ethical relativism claims that what is right or wrong depends on a person's cultural membership. According to ethical relativism, none of us should expect the members of a different culture to have the same moral standards that we do. Nor should any of us expect that we can get them to agree to our moral standards. If there are ethical disagreements between different cultures, and if there seems to be no way to resolve these disagreements in a rational way, then the principle that ethical judgments are always agreement-seeking and fully universalizable would be incorrect. This is the challenge of ethical relativism.

Much of the motivation for adopting a relativist stance in ethics comes from the study of radically different cultures. Cultural anthropologists have shown that cultures differ drastically regarding the duties of members to their kin, on what members of the culture may eat and how they should eat it, on how and with whom people may have sexual relations, and on how people should worship a god or gods. Cultures also differ drastically in what they judge to be ethically permissible behavior. Some cultures practice polygamy, some countenance the killing of family members to preserve the family's honor, and some cultures regularly mutilate the genitals of young girls. In the face of widespread cross-cultural disagreements regarding ethical judgments, and in the absence of any method of resolving these ethical disagreements in a rational way, it may appear that ethical relativism is the appropriate philosophical theory of ethics.

Ethical relativism appears attractive because it seems to epitomize toleration for other cultures. In their imperial past, Europeans had little respect for the cultures that they colonized. Colonizers mostly assumed that their own moral beliefs were far superior to those of the aboriginal people whom they had conquered. Anthropologists, such as Margaret Mead, reacted against this cultural imperialism by formulating the doctrine of cultural relativism. The ethical beliefs of aboriginal people were just as true for the aboriginal people as the ethical beliefs of the anthropologists were for the anthropologists. Cultural relativism seemed the proper way to show respect for other cultures, and ethical relativism provided a philosophical justification for cross-cultural tolerance.

However, respect for and toleration of others does not require uncritical acceptance of their beliefs. Proper respect for others requires an engagement with their views. Each of us must take the views of others seriously, and not simply dismiss them as true-for-them but not true-for-us. We show respect for others only by taking their arguments seriously. No one takes the arguments of members of another culture seriously when he simply labels their arguments as true for people in that culture but not true for members of his culture. Ethical relativism can be a disguise for intellectual laziness and can, perhaps surprisingly, show disrespect for the views and arguments of members of other cultures.

There are also limitations to the idea that respecting other cultures implies our becoming ethical relativists. Some practices that are customary in other cultures are just too ghastly to tolerate. The killing of a young woman by her father and brothers to preserve the family honor is just wrong. Honor killing is wrong both for us and for members of that other culture. All of us should be more certain of the wrongness of honor killing than we are of the truth of ethical relativism. If ethical relativism implies that honor killing is ethically permissible in the other culture, then ethical relativism must be false.

Ethical relativism defines what is right or wrong according to the accepted practices of the culture of which someone is a member. Therefore, ethical relativism implies that if any member of the culture disagrees with the accepted practices of her culture, then her dissenting view is, by definition, false. If the accepted practices of a culture define what is right and wrong for its members, then how can people criticize their own culture's ethical practices? How can a member of an honor-killing culture criticize this accepted practice without contradicting herself? Ethical relativism potentially leads to an extremely strong cultural conservatism that makes cultural reform or cultural change ethically impossible. This position is incompatible with ethics in general. The essence of ethics is to think critically about our accepted moral practices. Ethics, as practiced by philosophers, does not merely describe the ethos of a culture and the mores of its members. It always subjects the accepted practices of a culture to critical reflection.

Ethical relativism assumes that the ethical beliefs and practices of a culture are homogeneous. This is unlikely to be the case. In any honor-killing culture, doubtlessly many members of the culture do not accept the practice. If cultures are internally diverse in their ethical beliefs, then how do we determine which of these ethical beliefs defines what is right and wrong for members of the culture? If we are to say that what is right or wrong is relative to cultural membership, then we need a way to determine which of a culture's ethical beliefs are authoritative for members of each culture. It is unlikely that we will be able to do so.

There is much genuine ethical disagreement in the world. Ethics is agreement-seeking, but not always agreement-finding. Sometimes people disagree because they have different beliefs about the facts of the case, sometimes because they hold different ethical theories, sometimes because they place different weights on the same ethical considerations, and sometimes because they come from different cultural backgrounds.

Ethical disagreement between cultures may not be as rampant as ethical relativists assume. Ethical disagreement about a specific case does not necessarily imply ethical disagreement at a deep level. The disagreement may be about the facts of the case, not the ethical principles involved. Consider the attempt by members of the Spanish Inquisition to use torture and execution to stamp out heresy during the Counter-Reformation in the sixteenth century. From our contemporary vantage point, we cannot immediately infer that the inquisitors had radically different ethical beliefs from our own, and that we believe in promoting human welfare whereas the inquisitors did not. The inquisitors had specific factual beliefs that are uncommon today. They believed in an afterlife that included eternal hell for heretics who did not repent, and they believed that coerced repentance was a way for heretics to avoid this hell. The inquisitors probably believed in the importance of human welfare, where avoiding hellish torment in the eternal afterlife easily outweighed some days of pain in this life. We can interpret the inquisitors as holding to principles regarding human welfare similar to those of contemporary people, but then see them as differing in their application of these principles because of their different beliefs regarding facts about the world.

In applying ethics to an inter-cultural difficulty, it is important to consider the cultural background of ourselves and others, because our various cultural backgrounds may affect the facts of the case. However, tolerance and respect for cultural diversity is best shown by respectful engagement with the opinions of others, not by uncritical acceptance of their views.

1.3 Exercises

1. Formulate a definition for ethical relativism and repeat the definition aloud to help you remember it.
2. Why are people tempted to be ethical relativists?
3. Summarize the Respect-Does-Not-Equal-Uncritical-Acceptance argument against ethical relativism.
4. Summarize the Too-Ghastly-to-Tolerate argument against ethical relativism.
5. Summarize the Ethical-Conservatism argument against ethical relativism.
6. Summarize the Non-Homogeneity argument against ethical relativism.
7. Summarize the Not-All-Disagreements-Are-Ethical argument against ethical relativism.

1.4 ETHICAL DECISION-MAKING

Applying ethics to the problem of living with others is made difficult by the complexity of ethical judgments. Ethical judgments are complex because in making ethical decisions each of us is trying to do three different things: (1) Each of us is trying to be a good person, (2) each of us is trying to act on principles that we believe to be the right way to treat others, and (3) each of us is trying to create moral value for ourselves and others.

If we are called on to judge the actions of another, then these three different general approaches lead to several questions. We make a judgment about the person performing the action: Is the person a virtuous person? We make a judgment about the motivations of this person: Is the person acting because of ethical principles that she believes to be correct? We make a judgment about the consequences of the person's chosen action: Does the action cause the most valuable results? And, we make a judgment about the recipients of these results: Are the others who are affected by the action entitled to moral consideration?

If we are lucky, then all these judgments will align with one another: A virtuous moral agent, doing right according to true moral principles, produces the best possible consequences for all those deserving to be considered from an ethical point of view. Unfortunately, however, these different aspects of an overall ethical judgment are not always in alignment. Different types of ethical consideration can point in different directions. An evil person may sometimes make a principled decision, or a person acting with wrong intent may produce wonderful results. The first step in making an overall judgment is identifying all the ethical considerations that need to be considered.

Ethical judgments typically arise in situations that involve (1) a moral agent (which could be a person, organization, or corporation) (2) making and implementing a decision that (3) results in consequences for some beneficiary or victim who is the (4) recipient of the consequences. Figure 1.3 shows schematically a typical situation to which an ethical judgment applies.

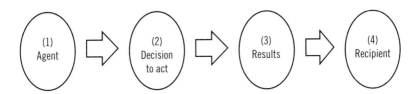

Figure 1.3: Components of a typical ethical judgment: A person or organization implements a decision that produces various consequences for one or more recipients.

A **moral agent** is an entity to whom we are prepared to assign praise or blame, who can understand moral principles, who can respond to moral reasons, and whom we hold morally accountable. Adult human beings are typically moral agents. A large question in business ethics, however, is whether an organization, a corporation, or a government department possesses moral agency, and whether we can hold them morally accountable. In animal and environmental ethics, we assume that animals or wilderness areas are not moral agents. In legal ethics, whether the judge should hold someone legally responsible for a crime or an injury is often a very important question.

Each component of an ethical situation requires a different theoretical approach. Ethical theories are attempts to systematize our ethical judgments with a small number of principles. There are three different types of ethical theory that we can classify by looking at a typical situation to which an ethical judgment applies. We can focus either on the character of the agent, on the principles that guide the decision to action, or on the benefits and harms of the consequences. Determinations of moral standing will depend on these theories.

A moral agent ...	... decides to perform an action ...	... that brings about consequences ...	... for some person or other organism.
Character? Identity? Good person?	Intentions? Motivations? Principles?	Benefits? Harms? Moral value?	Moral standing?

Table 1.1: Aspects of an overall moral decision.

We will call ethical theories that focus on the character of the agent, that evaluate the agent's character as either virtuous or vicious, and that assess what sort of person the agent is, **identity-based theories**. We will call ethical theories that focus on the intentions of the agent when the agent decides to act and that focus on the principles (such as performing a duty or respecting moral rights) that guide the decision, **principle-based theories**. We will call ethical theories that focus on the results of the decision and assess the consequences according to how much benefit or harm they produce, **consequence-based theories**. In applying ethics, it is important to learn to identify what sort of ethical theory moral agents rely on when they make a moral judgment. We will return to this classification scheme in more detail later.

In applying ethical theories to cases, we must ask whom or what the consequences affect, and whether the entity affected counts from a moral point of view. This raises the big question of which recipients of beneficial or harmful consequences we should care about from an ethical point of view. We know we should care about other people, and we know that we do not need to care about stones and piles of gravel, but it is more difficult to decide if we should care about animals, or about trees, or about human fetuses twelve weeks after conception, or about future generations of people who do not yet exist. An entity has moral standing, or some degree of moral status, if we must consider it, or its interests, when we are making an ethical judgment. An entity is morally considerable if the entity has moral standing. If an entity has **moral standing**, then we must be virtuous in behavior towards it, or we must think carefully about our duties towards it, or we must be careful about the consequences of our actions for its health or welfare.

We can already foresee a major problem for ethical reasoning. Assessing any ethical situation will involve attending to at least three different sorts of ethical considerations: character, principles, and results. It would be wonderful if these considerations always lined up so that either an admirable person following the right principles produced good results, or a despicable person following the wrong principles produced evil results. Unfortunately, some situations will involve a person of ordinary virtue whose intentions are good, but whose actions produce less than optimal consequences, or shady people with wrongful motivations whose actions produce beneficial unintended consequences. This is when ethical reasoning becomes difficult. Ethical principles involving persons, actions, and results can conflict with one another, and we will have to somehow balance these considerations when coming to an overall ethical judgment.

In applying ethics, we use ethical theories to provide a framework for thinking about specific ethical decisions. However, ethical theories do not provide an ethical code of conduct covering all decisions that might ever arise. Though there is no recipe for making good ethical decisions, the ethical decision-making process will have certain components:

1. Recognizing that an ethical decision is required
2. Deciding who is morally accountable for the decision
3. Identifying whose interests must be considered
4. Considering all the alternative courses of action
5. Identifying the relevant types of ethical reasoning
6. Categorizing this ethical reasoning according to the ethical theories being assumed
7. Distinguishing the ethically relevant facts of the case
8. Reflecting critically on the strengths and weaknesses of the ethical reasons being used
9. Balancing any conflicting ethical considerations
10. Making an overall decision

Ethical theory informs each of these components. Making an ethical decision involves considering alternative courses of action in the context of various ethical theories, and then bringing these ethical considerations together to decide on the overall best course of action. It would have been wonderful if deciding what to do was always as easy as just interpreting a gut reaction. However, some ethical decisions are extremely complicated and require consideration of many factors, many of which may conflict in their recommendations.

1.4 Exercises

1. Formulate definitions for each of the following and repeat each definition aloud to help you remember it: (a) moral agent, (b) identity-based ethical theory, (c) principle-based ethical theory, (d) consequence-based ethical theory, and (e) moral standing.
2. Give examples, different from those in the text, of (a) a being who is not a moral agent, (b) an identity-based ethical consideration, (c) a principle-based ethical consideration, (d) a consequence-based ethical consideration, and (d) a being whose moral standing is controversial.

1.5 IDENTITY, PRINCIPLE, AND CONSEQUENCE

Ethical theory enables us to observe the different sorts of ethical considerations that go into a decision. When we pass a beam of white light through a prism, the prism breaks the white light down into its component colors: red, orange, yellow, green, blue, and purple. The optical prism is a useful metaphor for the role of ethical theory (Crane & Matten 2004, 104).

We can make the metaphorical prism of ethical theory into a more precise observational tool by making exact distinctions between different types of ethical theory. We will begin here with a survey of the principal types of ethical theory. In later chapters we will discuss these types of ethical theory in much more detail, and further distinguish them into subtypes. To repeat, what follows is a brief, preliminary survey. Further chapters will cover the theories in more detail and make them more understandable.

1. IDENTITY-BASED ETHICAL THEORIES: The identity-based approach to ethical reasoning leads to ethical theories that assess the sort of person the moral agent has become. A **virtue ethics** holds that persons and organizations ought to cultivate a virtuous or morally excellent character. A **virtue** is a stable character trait with positive moral significance. Examples are courage, generosity, benevolence, and fairness. A **vice** is a stable character trait with

negative moral significance. Examples are avarice, cowardice, dishonesty, and sleaziness. A virtue ethics holds that both persons and organizations ought to cultivate a morally excellent character.

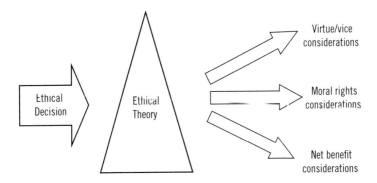

Figure 1.4: An ethical decision passes through the "prism" of ethical theory to reveal the different sorts of ethical considerations relevant to the decision.

If we understand the identity-based approach more widely so that it encompasses the nature of the agent, then we can think of a feminist ethics of care within this framework. Some feminist ethicists argue that the biological nature, upbringing, and education of women gives women a perspective on ethical decisions that is different from the dominant perspective of men. A feminist **care ethics** is concerned with establishing and preserving harmonious social relationships and with caring for others. This contrasts with traditional ethics, mostly developed by men, that tends to be concerned with following principles and calculating net benefits. A feminist care ethics, like a virtue ethics, emphasizes the role of discussion, wisdom, and judgment in ethical decisions and downplays the role of principles and calculations.

2. PRINCIPLE-BASED ETHICAL THEORIES: The principle-based approach to ethical reasoning says that each agent should be motivated by foundational ethical principles that are not derived from other types of ethical thinking. The qualification is important since any ethical advice can be formulated as an ethical principle. For example, virtue-based advice can be formulated as the principle, "Always act as a virtuous person would act," and consequence-based advice can be formulated as the principle, "Always create the maximum amount of moral value." Principle-based ethical theories, as the term is used here, are what philosophers call "deontological" theories, theories that are based on an account of moral duties that is independent of being a good person or creating moral value. An example of such an independent account

of duties is Kant's famous categorical imperative, which will be described below. There are several different types of principle-based ethical theories.

In **duty-based theories** of ethics, the agent should follow the principle of doing his or her duty, regardless of the consequences. An example is the set of duties imposed by the ten commandments in the Hebrew and Christian Bibles. These include both negative duties, such as "Thou shalt not kill," and positive duties, such as "Remember the sabbath day to keep it holy."

In **rights-based theories**, the moral principles that agents should follow in their decisions involve respecting the moral rights of others. Respecting the moral rights of others may include respecting their freedom to do as they wish without coercing them into doing otherwise, respecting their autonomous choices without trying to manipulate them, or respecting their private property rights to use things that they own in ways that they choose.

In **justice-based theories**, the moral principles that agents should follow in their decisions involve treating others fairly. Treating others fairly requires treating everyone in the same way unless there are morally relevant reasons for treating them differently. Justice may require, for example, that businesses install access ramps for people with disabilities. Doing so treats some customers differently, but the different treatment is not morally arbitrary. Because some customers have disabilities that make using stairs impossible, there is a morally relevant reason for providing special ramps.

3. CONSEQUENCE-BASED ETHICAL THEORIES: In consequence-based approaches to ethical reasoning, what matters is that the outcome should be as good as possible. To use a cliché, the end justifies the means, when the end is the best end possible. The goodness of the end can be measured in several ways, each giving rise to a different type of consequentialist theory. If we value the outcome of the decision as a good state of the world, then we have an objective form of consequentialism. **Non-psychological consequentialism** requires agents to make those decisions which lead to the best consequences from a point of view that is independent of the psychological states of individual people. For example, someone might claim that the international prestige of her nation is a good thing whether or not it makes citizens happier, and that maximizing her nation's international prestige should be a goal of ethical decision-making.

Non-psychological consequentialism contrasts with forms of utilitarianism, which judge the goodness of outcomes purely in terms of the positive and negative psychological states that they bring about. Psychological consequentialism or **utilitarianism** requires agents to make those decisions which maximize positive mental states in both themselves and others. The original developers of utilitarianism thought that ethical decisions should aim at producing the maximum amount of human happiness, which they equated with pleasure and the absence of pain. Modern versions often talk of ethical decisions aiming to bring about the greatest amount of satisfied preferences. Modern economics is a descendent of utilitarian thinking. Economists have shown that markets in perfect competition are optimal for satisfying people's preferences. We will later look critically at the economic utilitiarian justification for the free-market system.

Another type of consequence-based ethical theory is ethical egoism. **Ethical egoism** is the ethical theory that agents ought always to maximize only their own self-interest. Ethical egoists believe that they should strive for results that maximize their own happiness, pleasure, or preference satisfaction. Ethical egoism is an ethical theory and not a psychological theory. It is not the empirical hypothesis, sometimes accepted in economic theory, that rational agents always *do* make choices that maximize the satisfaction of their own preferences. It is the ethical theory that moral agents always *should* make choices that maximize the satisfaction of their own preferences.

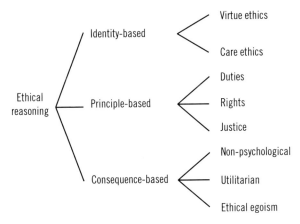

Figure 1.5: A preliminary taxonomy of ethical theories classified according to the different types of ethical reasoning involved.

We now have a preliminary theoretical framework into which we can put many of the considerations that come up in making an ethical decision. This theoretical framework will help us to think about the ethical decisions that we must make. We can also use it as a sort of checklist that will help prevent us from neglecting any important ethical considerations. This section has introduced a larger number of ethical theories than anyone could be expected to understand and remember at one time. We will return repeatedly to these various theories, and each time they will become clearer.

1.5 Exercises

1. Formulate definitions for each of the following and repeat each definition aloud to help you remember it: (a) virtue ethics, (b) care ethics, (c) moral duty, (d) moral rights, (e) justice, (f) non-psychological consequentialism, (g) utilitarianism, and (h) ethical egoism.

2. Classify the type of ethical reasoning implicit in the following examples, and briefly explain why the reasoning fits this classification:
    a) A trainee manager finds that she must work 100 hours a week, compete all the time with fellow managers, and be overly aggressive with employees. She worries about the sort of person she is becoming.
    b) A trainee manager finds that he must work 100 hours a week, compete all the time with fellow managers, and be overly aggressive with employees. He worries about how this will affect his family life, his friendships at work, and the collegiality of his workplace.
    c) A Muslim shopkeeper refuses to charge interest on overdue customer accounts.
    d) An NGO campaigns to stamp out sexual abuse in the film industry.
    e) Polluters should pay.
    f) Governments should strive to maximize the production of scientific knowledge.
    g) Governments should approach environmental problems by considering what would maximize human welfare.
    h) People should look after themselves first.

CHAPTER 2

BEING A GOOD PERSON

ETHICALLY PROBLEMATIC SITUATIONS TYPICALLY INVOLVE A DECISION-maker, her various motives, and the results of her decision. This leads to three broad types of ethical reasoning and three different ethical questions. Would a good person make the sort of decision contemplated? Does the decision employ principles that are in accord with moral duty? And lastly, will the decision result in the creation of what is morally valuable?

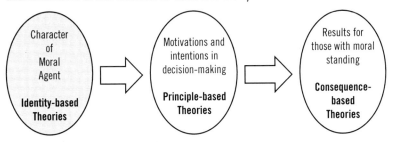

Figure 2.1: Categories of ethical theories. A person with a virtuous or vicious character is motivated by his or her principles to implement a decision that produces good or bad consequences for others.

Because there are three independent types of moral reasoning, each with a different subject matter—character, principle, or consequence—the ethical theories that correspond to each subject matter can lead to different conclusions about how to act. Unfortunately, admirable people do not always follow sound principles and produce valuable results. Nor do despicable people always follow false principles that lead them to create evil. Different categories of ethical theory sometimes offer different advice as to how to evaluate an action. To make matters worse, there are variations within the above three categories of ethical theory. For example, one theory of value creation might advise maximizing overall pleasure, another might advise maximally satisfying everyone's desires, and yet another might suggest maximizing the financial income received by everyone. To usefully apply ethics to a problematic situation a decision-maker needs to bring these considerations together into an all-things-considered decision.

A good way to make an all-things-considered decision is to use the advice of all varieties of ethical theorizing to reveal the morally relevant features of a case, and then to balance the strengths and weaknesses of these considerations into an overall decision. The following chapters will cover the various categories and sub-categories of ethical theory in more detail. This will show how the theories apply, show the strengths and weaknesses of the theories, and show how to balance them into an all-things-considered decision.

This chapter examines ethical theories concerning the nature or identity of the decision-maker. Historically, theories of how to be a good person were the first ethical theories to be developed. Virtue ethics dates to the Ancient Greek and Ancient Chinese philosophers. We will look first at how a person of good character, a virtuous person, a morally excellent person, would make decisions in a problematic situation. We will then look at how a caring and loving person would make ethical decisions. Figure 2.2 shows how virtue ethics and care ethics fit into a conceptual map of ethical theories.

Figure 2.2: Conceptual map showing virtue ethics and care ethics as identity-based ethical theories.

Lastly, we will look at the theory of justice that goes with a virtue ethics. This is a theory of justice in which people get the rewards they deserve based on their moral virtue, and the punishments that they deserve based on their vices.

2.1 VIRTUE ETHICS

Vices are stable character traits with negative moral significance, while **virtues** are stable character traits with positive moral significance. Virtues are forms of moral excellence. There is no sharp distinction between the excellences with little moral significance that are simply skills and the excellences with large moral significance that are the moral virtues. Fairness and honesty obviously carry high levels of positive moral significance whereas shrewdness and persistence carry less. Moral virtues tend to foster social cooperation in almost every interpersonal situation in a society, whereas non-moral excellences and skills tend to be more self-centered and less universal.

Our excellences and virtues are part of who we are. For each of us, our virtues are part of our identity as individual human beings. Acting virtuously, we prove what type of person we are. We confirm ourselves to be honest, trustworthy, and fair. Acting contrary to virtue, we demonstrate our vices. We confirm ourselves to be dishonest, untrustworthy, or unjust.

Virtues and vices are not conscious mental states like pain or pleasure, nor are they mental processes, such as rational calculations or applications of ethical principles. They are skills, traits, or dispositions. Because they are dispositions, we can talk meaningfully and non-metaphorically about the virtues of nation states, societies, communities, and corporations.

Virtue appears in applied ethics in two different ways. One way understands the virtues as basic to ethical theory. Another way understands the virtues as serving the purposes of other principle- or consequence-based ethical theories. **Derivative virtues** are character traits that are justified because they help an agent fulfill the requirements of some other type of ethical theory.

Virtues are stable character traits that enable human beings and organizations to flourish in cooperation with others who have similar or complementary traits. Understanding virtue requires understanding the notions of character traits, of human flourishing, and of a social cooperation.

Character traits are enduring dispositions to consistently behave in certain ways in relevant circumstances. They are habits that we acquire through upbringing, education, self-discipline, and practice. To be virtuous, it is not enough to perform just one good action. One donation to charity is not enough to make a person generous. Nor is a strategy of acting well for personal gain an indication of virtue. Adopting honesty as the best policy does not make a person an honest sort of person. Generous people are disposed to repeatedly share with the needy and honest people want to tell the truth, even when it is inconvenient to do so.

People are perfectly virtuous if it is second nature for them do the right thing. Perfect virtue involves a form of moral perception; perfectly virtuous people "see" what they should do and then act on it. They do the right thing intuitively. In this, they are like skilled drivers who naturally make the right decisions in dangerous circumstances, or skilled hockey players who instantly make the best play.

To follow a virtue ethics rule of action is to emulate how a virtuous person would act in a problematic situation. People who are not perfectly virtuous, that is, most of us, can reason by imagining what someone whose moral excellence we admire—mothers, friends, bosses, business heroes, or religious leaders—would do in the situation that we face.

Vice	Virtue	Vice
Dishonesty	Honesty	Over-disclosure
Cowardice	Courage	Recklessness
Greed	Moderation	Self-sacrifice
Meanness	Generosity	Excessiveness
Unfairness	Justice	Rigidity
Disloyalty	Loyalty	Fanaticism

Table 2.1: A virtue is the mean between two vices: Some examples of the rich conceptual vocabulary available within virtue ethics.

Virtue also requires practical wisdom. Moral perceptiveness, the ability to "see" the relevant ethical issues in a situation, and moral competence, the ability to "see" what to do in response to these ethical issues, are both forms of wisdom that are not readily reduced to calculations of consequences or applications of principle. Wisdom is involved in the understanding of the various virtues and vices. A virtue is the mean between two vices, as courage is the mean between cowardice and recklessness. For example, it is generous for a person to make a reasonable donation to a charitable cause. However, a disposition towards offering too little would be greedy, while a disposition towards offering too much might be imprudent. An honest business selling a product should be frank about the qualities of that product and its manufacturing. Yet, to say too little would be dishonest, while to say too much would entail the disclosure of trade secrets. The boundaries between virtue and vice are not easy to determine and may differ among different roles in society. We must learn a certain skill in applying virtue concepts.

The idea that a virtue is a mean between two vices has received some criticism. For one thing, there seem to be counter-examples. Suppose someone wants to eat a healthful diet. Too little of eating healthfully is bad, but what is too much? Refusing a single spoonful of ice cream is not an excess of being healthful—it is not health-relevant at all. It has nothing to do with health. Perhaps what we should say is that the value of this idea is that it gives us a conceptual vocabulary for thinking about ethical decisions that is much richer than simple divisions into right and wrong, good and bad, or just and unjust.

Virtuous human beings can flourish in cooperation with others who have similar or complementary traits, though a virtuous person among the vicious might be better off vicious. The notion of **human flourishing**, as understood in virtue ethics, is quite different from the notion of happiness as commonly understood. Virtue ethics understands flourishing as objective happiness, a form of happiness that an objective observer of a person's life could assess. Happiness is commonly understood as subjective happiness, as pleasurable experiences and satisfied desires that only the person who has them can assess. In virtue ethics, a happy life is a good life, lived with virtues such as integrity, self-respect, and honesty. These virtues also contribute to the maintenance of happy social circumstances and to the flourishing of everyone in society.

Virtue ethics understands that the circumstances required for a flourishing life include both natural and social circumstances. Virtues, which enable people to cooperate for mutual advantage in society, are also required to create and sustain good social circumstances. A society where people are generally honest, trustworthy, and supportive is more likely to prosper and sustain the social conditions required for the flourishing of its members. The virtues have less effect on the natural conditions of a flourishing life. No amount of virtue or moral excellence will protect a person from cancer or heart disease. Good health is, in part, a matter of good luck. However, living in a well-developed society that can provide good health care to its members is a matter of social cooperation, which, in turn, depends on members of the society having the necessary cooperative virtues.

Applying virtue ethics to a problematic situation is difficult because there is no known virtue-ethics algorithm for making moral decisions. Being virtuous is a skill for which there is no recipe. Similarly, emulating a virtuous person in our actions is also a skill without a recipe. All we can do is start from an understanding of the common virtues and vices (generosity, dishonesty, trustworthiness, greed, etc.), and then somehow learn, with the help of others, to recognize moral virtue and vice when we see them, and to develop the character necessary to avoid vice and to act in accord with these virtues.

2.1 Exercises

1. Formulate a definition for each of the following and repeat the definition aloud to help you remember it: (a) virtue, (b) vice, (c) derivative virtues, and (d) human flourishing.
2. Give three examples, different from those in the text, of (a) virtues and (b) vices.
3. Summarize, in your own words, why a virtuous person requires practical wisdom.
4. Summarize, in your own words, the distinction between the natural and social circumstances of a flourishing life.

2.2 VIRTUE, COOPERATION, AND COMMUNITY MEMBERSHIP

Some ancient virtue theorists, the Stoics, thought that all that is necessary for someone's life to be well-lived is for her to be perfectly virtuous. Circumstances do not matter; even a life of extreme privation is a flourishing life so long as it exemplifies the virtues. Other ancient virtue theorists, the Aristotelians, thought that circumstances do matter, and even a life that exemplified all the virtues could be a bad one due to unfortunate circumstances. Here, we will follow the Aristotelians and examine how the virtues contribute to creating and sustaining the circumstances in which people flourish. Two sorts of social circumstances are relevant to the flourishing. The first are social conditions: the preservation and development of the social practices, institutions, and communities that honor and reward people's virtues. The second are material conditions: the provision of those things, such as education, health care, insurance, and economic goods and services, which enable people's lives to flourish.

People who live in a community that inculcates virtue can avoid the dilemmas of cooperation afflicting people motivated only by self-interest. For example, in the Prisoner's Dilemma Game, two rational actors, motivated only by unenlightened self-interest, will each find that their best strategy is to cheat, no matter whether the other actor cheats or cooperates. The outcome of a Prisoner's Dilemma situation will be a less-than-optimal payoff for both players. However, people who live in communities that inculcate and sustain virtues of fidelity, trustworthiness, and reciprocity will achieve optimal outcomes. They can trust one another to keep their promises and can rely on cooperative behavior from each other. Virtues are permanent character traits; people do not suddenly behave out of character, so virtuous people can predict one another's behavior accurately. As virtuous people who know each other to be virtuous, they will dare to take the cooperative strategy, and they will flourish.

Having overcome the dilemmas of social cooperation, virtuous people still face the problem of dividing the gains from cooperation. Even if both parties are better off than they would be working alone, there could still be a division of the gains from their cooperation that is patently unfair. Unfair divisions can lead to resentment and anger and to the breakdown of cooperation. To reach a fair division, virtuous people need a sense of justice, a disposition to propose and accept fair divisions of the gains of cooperation.

Of course, villains can still free ride on the virtues of others. Widespread exercise of the virtues of moderation, truthfulness, fidelity, trustworthiness, and courage is required to realize the gains from social cooperation, but universal exercise of these virtues is not. One person without these traits may seize for himself an unfair share of the material gains from cooperation without compromising the general prevalence of cooperative behavior. An important virtue in these circumstances is the widespread courage to call attention to and to discourage such greedy, dishonest, unfaithful, untrustworthy, and reckless behavior.

Virtue ethics emphasizes the social context of an individual's life. Virtue ethics begins from two foundational assumptions: Individuals are already cooperating in a society and the flourishing of each individual depends on that individual's ability to work well with other members of the community. Moral virtues are character traits that enable community members to work together effectively. Not every society or community enables the flourishing of its members. For example, we can imagine a nasty society, whose members are impoverished and oppressed, and in which people must be dishonest and untrustworthy to survive. Such a society would encourage the vices and its members would not enjoy any gains from cooperation.

The virtues have their role in creating and maintaining a prosperous and just society that rewards and honors the virtues that sustain it. All communities require virtues of honesty, fidelity, and so on, for members to flourish. The virtues relate intimately to specific communities and to the social practices of their members. Virtues are skills in making ethical decisions that children learn within communities. Communities provide moral education in virtue. Adults may ultimately modify or reject the virtues that they learn as children, but childhood moral training provides the foundation for adult moral excellence. Communities sustain the virtues that they teach by honoring and sometimes rewarding virtue and by despising and punishing vice.

At the same time, the virtues inculcated by a community sustain the forms of social cooperation that make the community work. The relationship between virtue and community is reciprocal, as shown in Figure 2.3. The virtues enable social cooperation and therefore the existence of communities, while communities simultaneously inculcate, reward, and enable the practice of the various virtues.

Figure 2.3: A community teaches virtue to its members and enables them to exercise these virtues, while at the same time, the exercise of virtues of honesty, fidelity, and justice by community members sustains the social cooperation required for the existence of the community.

The gains from cooperation are twofold. In virtue ethics, a flourishing human life requires both economic goods and services and the exercise of the virtues. A good life requires a good set of social circumstances and the possession of a good character. Social cooperation provides community members with economic gains. This is one type of gain from social cooperation. Social cooperation also creates the type of community in which members can exercise the virtues whose possession is part of what it is to flourish and lead a good life. This is another type of gain from social cooperation and is a gain that is internal to the cooperation itself.

Because of the intimate, mutually supportive relationship of virtue to community, virtuous people acquire obligations simply through their membership in a community (Sandel 2009). For example, we have specific obligations to members of our families that we did not initially choose. We were born or adopted into these obligations. These are not general obligations, owed to everyone, that arise from obligations to promote the general welfare, and they are not general duties to respect the rights of others. Nor are they the specific obligations that people take on by voluntarily signing contracts with one another. Instead, the obligations of community membership are non-voluntary, specific obligations that people have because of their membership in a mutually sustaining family, community, or society. Virtuous people acknowledge obligations of loyalty and solidarity to fellow community members, and virtuous communities acknowledge similar obligations to the larger communities of which they are a part.

The obligations of community membership are not always overriding obligations. For example, a boss should not promote a family member over a more deserving employee; to do so would be nepotism. Nevertheless, the fact that the relative is a family member is still an ethical consideration in the decision. It is just that other ethical considerations such as fairness and employee rights outweigh the ethical obligations of family membership.

In applying virtue ethics to a morally problematic situation, we must pay attention to the society in which the situation occurs. We need to examine what virtues are required generally by membership in that society, and what virtues are required by persons with different roles in that society. For example, the roles of doctor, manager, parent, lawyer, sibling, therapist, home-maker, and assembly-line worker all give rise to specific sets of moral obligations and require somewhat different types of moral character. No decision-maker is morally perfect, so it is sometimes easier to evaluate the character of a decision-maker by looking for any vices that she exemplifies.

2.2 Exercises

1. Summarize, in your own words, how virtuous people can avoid the dilemmas of cooperation.
2. What would be the results of an Ultimatum Game played between two virtuous people? Why?
3. Summarize, in your own words, how virtues sustain a community and a community sustains virtue.
4. Summarize, in your own words, why virtuous community members have obligations to which they have not explicitly consented.

2.3 WISDOM AND VIRTUE

Virtues are prosocial character traits. They are stable dispositions to behave in a way that will enable a society of people with similar traits to cooperate with one another. In this, the virtues are like the prosocial emotions. The prosocial emotions enable people to cooperate, but do not determine the system of morality that will govern their interactions. The details of the system of morality are left as the subject of rational deliberation. Similarly, virtues also enable cooperation, but details of the system of prosocial virtues are left to the determination of other sorts of virtue, such as reason and wisdom. Because of this, ancient virtue theorists often treated wisdom as the highest virtue. The virtue of wisdom is required to make a system of cooperation into a fair and just system of cooperation. Wisdom is required to see how to balance the prosocial virtues into a harmonious whole.

One issue faced by the virtue ethics approach is accounting for the great diversity of character traits that different communities have praised as virtues. Homer praised the ferocity, reckless courage, and exaggerated sense of personal honor of Bronze Age warriors during the siege of Troy. The Ancient Greek philosopher, Aristotle, praised the speeches and public service of those who contributed to Athenian democracy, while not only accepting, but justifying, the ownership of slaves and the oppression of women and animals. The New Testament of the Christian bible stresses the virtues of faith, hope, charity, and meekness. The Victorians stressed the virtue of chastity, while often condoning adultery. Virtues and vices are relative to community standards, and the standards of some communities are highly questionable.

This raises the question of whether virtue ethics is a form of ethical relativism. Different communities, with different cultures, teach, praise, and reward different virtues. Further, even when communities appear to value the same virtues, they may have different interpretations of what it means to have that virtue. For example, courage meant something different to a Bronze Age warrior than it does to a twenty-first century social activist. Therefore, it seems that virtue is relative to culture. Someone might defend virtue ethics against the charge of cultural relativism by pointing out that cultures teach virtues to foster social cooperation, and the circumstances in which people are trying to cooperate differ. For example, in the barbaric times of the Trojan War, a community needed to teach warrior virtues to defend itself against outside aggression and so protect internal cooperation. Deciding whether all virtues have the same purpose—fostering social cooperation in society—in diverse historical circumstances would require extensive empirical investigation.

Some forms of virtue ethics may imply cultural conservatism as well as cultural relativism. Virtues are character traits, which are dispositions to behave. Virtues are not conscious decisions. Someone who is perfectly virtuous does the right thing automatically, without critical reflection. If virtues are merely unreflective dispositions to behave that a community inculcates and sustains, then it is difficult to see how community members can have the intellectual resources to take any sort of critical perspective on the virtues that they exercise automatically. If community standards are less than perfect, then how can community members reform their community from within? Reform of a community's standards from within is only possible if the community also inculcates the intellectual virtues required for critical reflection on those standards. A community needs to educate its members in the skills of critical thinking, the traits of skepticism, and the intellectual abilities of discussion and debate. Only a critical, skeptical community with an open forum for deliberation about the nature of virtue can develop and change from within.

The principal critics of virtue ethics and its communitarian background have been liberal philosophers such as Locke, Kant, and Mill. They have worried that the creation of virtuous community members is incompatible with the values of liberty and autonomy. For example, John Stuart Mill's Harm Principle forbade society to interfere with people for their own good or to make them into better, more virtuous citizens, and Mill railed against the way social pressure made people conform to community standards. Liberals worry that communities of virtue will brainwash members into a common conception of the good life. Liberals also worry that communitarians will too readily sacrifice the rights of individuals for the good of the community. For example, Hitler's fascists in the 1930s and 1940s sacrificed the human rights of Jews and other minority groups in the cause of creating an ethnically pure German community. The idea that community membership can be a source of ethical obligations must be tempered with the idea that respect for rights and justice will frequently override community obligations.

Critics of virtue ethics worry, too, about the vagueness of character traits as guides to ethical action. Other approaches appear to give guidance that is more precise. For example, Jeremy Bentham offered the overarching goal of producing the greatest net pleasure against which all other principles could be measured. Virtue ethics offers no such principle. The closest thing it can offer is the virtue ethics rule of action, which is to emulate the actions of a virtuous person, still imprecisely defined. On closer inspection, however, other ethical approaches are also vague in their implementation. For example, applying Bentham's pleasure-maximizing principle requires sensitivity to the experiences of others and learned insight into what will happen to people's experiences in response to various courses of action. If Bentham's utilitarian principle requires people to develop the character traits of benevolence, sensitivity, and causal insight for them to implement the principle, then his utilitarianism cannot be any more precisely defined than are the virtues of benevolence, sensitivity, and insight. If the other ethical approaches each require their own specific derivative virtues, then none of them can be any more precise than is virtue ethics itself.

Lastly, virtue ethics faces the problem of multiple community memberships. What virtues people should have will depend on which communities they are members of. Different communities often require different interpretations of the virtues. People are simultaneously members of different communities. Therefore, people often face the problem of integrating incompatible character traits. For example, the type of honesty that a salesperson requires in her role at work may differ considerably from the type of honesty that is appropriate to her role in the life of her family. As a salesperson, she will be disposed to disclose as much positive and as little negative information as she can legitimately get away with, whereas as someone's life partner, she may be disposed to disclose as much information as possible, positive or negative. Balancing work and home life is a problem that everyone faces. Similarly, for example, when Confucian virtues conflict with business virtues for a Chinese business executive, it may be difficult to integrate the two interpretations without considerable rationalization.

The Ancient Greek philosopher Aristotle (384–322 BCE) illustrates the potential relativity of an understanding of virtue to a specific society, culture, and historical epoch. In accord with the beliefs of his community, Aristotle thought that only those organisms that possessed the psychological capacity for reasoning had moral standing. He thought that no animal possessed reason, and that, therefore, no animals have moral standing. As is obvious in the passage below, he also thought that women and human slaves were devoid of the ability to reason, a claim that seems crazy to contemporary people.

> And it is clear that the rule of the soul over the body, and of the mind and the rational element over the passionate, is natural and expedient; whereas the equality of the two or the rule of the inferior is always hurtful. The same holds good of animals in relation to men; for tame animals have a better nature than wild, and all tame animals are better off when they are ruled by man; for then they are preserved. Again, the male is by nature superior, and the female inferior; and the one rules, and the other is ruled; this principle, of necessity, extends to all mankind. Where then there is such a difference as that between soul and body, or between men and animals (as in the case of those whose business is to use their body, and who can do nothing better), the lower sort are by nature slaves, and it is better for them as for all inferiors that they should be under the rule of a master. (Aristotle 350 BCE: *Politics*, Book I, Part V)

Aristotle uncritically accepts the ideology of his own society, whose consensus was that male speakers of Greek possessed the virtues of rationality and wisdom, whereas female speakers of Greek, non-Greek-speaking slaves, and non-speaking animals did not.

Virtues are character traits that both enable people to flourish within specific societies and enable these societies to endure and prosper for the good of their members. When we apply virtue ethics, we must be careful not to uncritically accept the moral beliefs of a specific society. Looking back in time from our modern point of view, we can easily think critically about Aristotle's slave-owning democracy or Homer's warrior society. It is much more difficult to think critically about the conceptual framework of our own society. A capitalist market society like ours inculcates virtues of prudence, honesty, and personal responsibility that in turn support the existence of that society. Different roles in a market society carry with them their own sets of virtues; the unbounded self-interest required of stockholders is quite different from the diligent acquiescence required of low-level employees. As members of a market society, it is easy to take for granted that these character traits are moral virtues. Yet, skillfully applying ethical concepts to situations requires us to reflect critically on what character traits we are calling moral virtues and why we are doing so.

2.3 Exercises

1. Summarize, in your own words, why inculcating the virtue of critical thinking is necessary for societies to avoid cultural conservatism.
2. Summarize, in your own words, the main liberal criticism of virtue ethics and community standards for virtue.
3. Give an example, different from the one in the text, of a society that inculcates character traits that you think are vices.

2.4 CARE ETHICS

There is widespread acceptance of the view that women's moral development and women's moral decision-making is different from that of men. It is mostly men's patterns of moral decision-making that are represented in traditional ethical theory. In her ground-breaking study of women's moral development, *In a Different Voice*, Carol Gilligan argued that women have a different conception of moral decision-making than do men.

> In this conception, the moral problem arises from conflicting responsibilities rather than from competing rights and requires for its resolution a mode of thinking that is contextual and narrative rather than formal and abstract. This conception of morality as concerned with the activity of care centers moral development around the understanding of responsibility and relationships, just as the conception of morality as fairness ties moral development to the understanding of rights and rules. (Gilligan 1982, 19)

Some feminists have embraced this difference and have argued in favor of an ethics of care. A care ethic incorporates into ethical decision-making both caring for less powerful others and nurturing important relationships.

Care ethics is an ethics based in the special relationships, such as that of mother and child, which people have to one another. It focuses on the relationship skills and emotional traits that make such attachments possible. It is an identity-based feminism, affirming the historical differences between men's and women's ethical reasoning and arguing that these create an alternative feminist standpoint in ethics. Childbearing, motherhood, and care for dependents have, in the past, given women a special perspective on ethical decision-making. Care ethics recognizes that these relationships are relationships of unequal power but insists that they should not give rise to subordination. Care ethics recommends that such aspects of human relations be applied by both men and women to their relationships with others.

We cannot formulate care ethics in a simple principle such as, "Act always to produce the maximum human happiness." In this respect, care ethics is like virtue ethics. It emphasizes the teaching and learning of ethical skills, traits of character, and emotional responses that are required to nurture human relationships. Relationship to others is vital to a human life. Human beings can neither grow nor thrive in the absence of relationships to others. Creating and sustaining such relationships requires skill, attention, and a set of appropriate attitudes and dispositions. A care ethic brings these traits from family life into society-at-large. It will include at least three components.

First, care ethics emphasizes moral perception. It suggests that decision-makers should learn and cultivate sensitivity to the needs of others and to the nature of the relationships between people. This means developing a nuanced sensitivity to the individual particularity of real people, not just an abstract understanding of the common humanity of human beings. Practitioners of care ethics will perceive the emotional needs and hurts of others and not simply treat them as autonomous, rational, utility maximizers. They will examine the whole context of the ethical situation instead of creating a simplified model of the situation that would abstract from its details so that it readily falls under some principle or other. They will discern the contextual differences between ethical situations rather than look only for the similarities that would enable them to apply abstract ethical principles to the case. Practitioners of care ethics will cultivate the virtues of moral sensitivity and discernment.

Second, care ethics emphasizes concern for responsibilities to others and a concern for relationships with others. Practitioners of care ethics will be disposed to nurture the quality of both their own relationships and those of others. They will see life as about cooperation and reciprocity, not about conflict and competition. Therefore, they will focus on strengthening and sustaining social cooperation rather than on respecting rights, applying principles of justice, or calculating how to maximize happiness.

Third, care ethics emphasizes particularistic moral reasoning. This means that practitioners of the ethics of care will not dismiss their relationships to specific people because such relationships detract from the impartiality of their ethical reasoning. We have seen that shared community membership gives virtuous people special obligations to fellow community members. These ethical obligations exist, even though they do not override all other considerations in ethical reasoning. Similarly, caring relationships give practitioners of the ethics of care special obligations to specific others. This results in a partiality of concern that practitioners must balance against other ethical considerations. Care ethics requires the cultivation and application of the virtues both of caring and of wisdom. Balancing care for special relationships against other ethical reasons requires ethical judgment that is more than just the application of principles, the calculation of utilities, or even the cultivation of virtues of fairness and impartiality.

Care ethics contrasts with traditional ethics in several ways. First, it conflicts with the concern of standard ethical theories for impartiality. Traditional theories are universal in scope and apply their recommendations to everyone equally. It is the very essence of justice that fair decisions treat everyone the same unless there are morally relevant grounds for treating them differently. Yet, as we have seen, the ethics of care abandons total impartiality and makes us balance our special responsibilities against our concern for impartial justice. Care ethics reminds us that special relationships sometimes provide morally relevant grounds for being partial in our decisions. Consider a case where a woman sees two children drowning in a pool. She does not have time to save them both. One of them is her son and the other is unknown to her. She decides to save her son. Her special relationship to her son and her special responsibilities for her son give her morally relevant reasons for deciding to save him rather than the unknown child. The ethics of care calls our attention to important and morally relevant considerations. On the other hand, it is important for a care ethic to avoid nepotism. For example, a parent should not try to influence a teacher to give her child extra advantages that other children in the class do not receive. In the work world, special relationships based on family and friendship can conflict with treating others as moral equals in the distribution of positions and rewards. Balancing care against justice is a difficult task requiring experience and wisdom.

Secondly, it is difficult to see how to extend an ethics of care to people in distant countries (or to people in future generations) with whom we have no relationships. It is easier for ethical theories based on universal and impartial moral consideration to look after the interests of distant or future people than it is for ethical theories based on special relationships to specific people. This objection applies most strongly to the idea that a feminist ethic of care should replace standard ethics. The objection applies only weakly to the idea that a care ethic provides us with reasons to care for special people, reasons that we must balance against other impartial reasons of fairness and respect for human rights generally.

Thirdly, it is difficult for an ethics of care to define just how much care we owe to others. A caretaker must care both for others and for herself. How much care is appropriate for others and how much for herself? A justice-based approach offers a ready solution; a caregiver is entitled to a fair share, just as others are. An alternative interpretation sees a care ethic as parallel to a virtue ethic. A virtue is often a mean between two vices. For example, courage is the mean between cowardice and recklessness.

Cowardice	Courage	Recklessness

Figure 2.4: Courage is the mean between cowardice and recklessness.

In virtue ethics, we require practical wisdom to determine when courage becomes foolish recklessness on one side, and when courage becomes weak fearfulness on the other. Similarly, care is the mean between selfishness and self-sacrifice.

Selfishness	Care	Self-sacrifice

Figure 2.5: Care is the mean between selfishness and self-sacrifice.

The practitioner of care ethics requires practical wisdom as well as a sense of justice to determine the boundaries between care and selfishness and between care and self-sacrifice.

A care ethic incorporates caring for less powerful others, and nurturing important relationships, into ethical decision-making. In applying the insights of care ethics, the question arises of whether care ethics should replace other forms of ethics or just supplement them. In keeping with our ethically pluralist approach, we will adopt the latter approach. We will employ considerations drawn from care ethics that can help us make better decisions in ethical matters.

2.4 Exercises

1. Summarize, in your own words, how care ethics differs from a standard ethical theory such as utilitarianism.
2. Summarize, in your own words, the three aspects of ethical decision-making that are emphasized by care ethics.
3. Give an example of a case where care-ethics considerations appear to conflict with the impartiality of justice.
4. Summarize, in your own words, why it is difficult for care ethics to aid decision-making about our generation's obligations to unborn members of future generations.

2.5 JUSTICE AND VIRTUE

Morality is about creating and sustaining a system of social cooperation through moral suasion. Moral suasion involves the apportioning of praise and blame to actions. Virtuous, trusting, and trustworthy people can avoid sub-optimal outcomes in cooperation problems, such as the Prisoner's Dilemma, and can reap the gains of cooperation. This brings up a new problem: The gains from cooperating must be distributed in a way that is fair and just. In the original example of Gog and Magog, both cooperators ended up with the same amount of satisfaction. However, in a different situation one of them could have ended up with more than the other. The one with less might have complained that, even though he was better off than if he had started a fight, he was still treated unfairly. After all, he might claim, he had exhibited the virtues of trustworthiness and cooperation to the same extent the other guy did. It is a short step from praising and blaming people to distributing the gains of cooperation to them in a way that rewards their cooperation and punishes their defections. We will examine what virtue ethics says about a just system of reward and punishment.

We treat all those with moral standing fairly when we treat them as moral equals. Treating persons as moral equals implies treating them in the same way, unless we have a good reason to treat them differently. The agreement-seeking aspect of ethical reasoning implies that we must always stand ready to offer justifications for our claims about just treatment. The practice of reason giving implies that adequate justifications for moral claims should be considerations that are morally relevant and not morally arbitrary. It is unjust to reserve convenient parking spaces for white people, but it is perfectly fair to reserve them for people in wheelchairs. Race is a morally arbitrary reason for treating people differently, whereas being in a wheelchair is a morally relevant consideration. From the perspective of virtue ethics, virtue and vice are morally relevant reasons for treating people differently. Those who pillage, rape, and murder are surely vicious people deserving of punishment. Those who work diligently and honestly for the good of the community are surely virtuous people deserving of reward.

As we saw, it is not only the case that virtuous people sustain cooperation in a society, but also the case that society educates its members in virtue. A system of reward for virtue and punishment for vice is built into the education of community members. Schools reward children for studying hard and parents reward them for sitting quietly when visiting Grandma. Schools punish children with bad grades for not studying and parents punish them with time-outs for screaming and shouting in Grandma's living room. Reward and punishment have a role in educating people in virtue. For virtue ethics, a natural suggestion is that a just system is one where community members get what they deserve, and where their desert is based on their moral virtues and vices. Notice, however, that a person who works for the good of the community because of hopes of this reward is not a truly virtuous person leading a life that flourishes according to virtue theory. The pretense of virtue in the hopes of reward is not true virtue.

The theory that justice is desert based on virtue has weaknesses as well as strengths. One weakness of the theory is its cultural relativity. The virtues required by the members of warrior societies, such as the little kingdoms of Homeric Greece, were very different from the virtues required of members of a market society such as our own. Warrior societies reward character traits such as ferocity, aggressiveness, physical valor, and a larger-than-life sense of honor, whereas market societies reward character traits such as diligence, prudence, success, and personal responsibility. Even where the two types of society ostensibly valorize the same character trait, say courage, the trait means something different in the two societies. The reckless physical courage of a warrior is very different from the calculated risk-taking of a courageous investor in a volatile stock market. Therefore, on a theory of justice according to virtue or vice, rewards and punishments will be distributed differently in different cultures.

To make an ethical judgment regarding the fairness of a system of rewards and punishments in a society, we thus need to evaluate the character traits of the cultures themselves. A character trait is a stable disposition to behave in specific ways in specific circumstances, so it is possible for an organization that does not have a mental life, such as a business corporation, a university, or a society, to be said to have character traits. By analogy to the characters of individual humans, we might say that the character traits of societies are virtues if they enable these societies to cooperate with one another. According to that standard, the virtues of a market society are apparently superior to the virtues of a warrior society because market societies tend to engage in free trade, whereas warrior societies tend to engage in war and conquest. Yet, just because a market society is ethically superior to a warrior society, it does not follow that a market society is beyond criticism; there may be alternatives that are better, but which suggest rewarding yet another set of more advanced virtues.

Another problem with thinking of justice as rewarding virtue is a tendency for societies to be arbitrary in how they select the virtues that they reward. Good parenting is essential to cooperative behavior in both warrior and market societies, yet the virtues of the good parent receive little social reward in either society. Perhaps this is because the leaders of these societies—heroic warriors or successful businessmen—tend to organize their societies so that the virtues rewarded are the virtues that they themselves display, and the virtues forgotten are the equally important ones of the less powerful. We, however, should think critically about how our society selects specific virtues for reward.

The problem is to say how much reward or punishment is appropriate to the virtuous and to the vicious. Proportionality is important here. Sentencing a child who steals candy from the convenience store to the guillotine would clearly be inappropriate, as would allowing a few successful businessmen to expropriate all the gains from economic cooperation. The obvious answer to this question is to say that a virtuous person's reward should be proportional to her contribution to her society. However, there are difficulties with both identifying and measuring someone's contribution to society. Suppose that there are two people in a Prisoner's Dilemma situation who, by cooperating, can move from a total joint payoff of $1,000 to a total payoff of $3,000. This produces a net $2,000 gain from cooperating. Who deserves the $2,000 in gains from cooperation? She might argue that she deserves the entire $2,000 because she caused the existence of these gains; if she had not cooperated, then the $2,000 gain would not exist. But he could make the same argument; but for his cooperation, the gain would not exist either. Disentangling individual contributions to even a simple collective endeavor can be next to impossible, and most schemes of social cooperation are far more complicated than this one.

In this simple situation there at least existed a common measure of contribution, which is financial gain. In other cases, contributions are of different types and cannot be measured against one another. The contribution to society of a good mother who raises a family of virtuous children cannot be measured against the contribution of a manager who helps run a large corporation employing many people; the two types of contribution are incommensurable, and just rewards are not calculable.

Earlier we noticed that a system of rewards and punishments is essential to educating members of a society in the required virtues and to keeping them virtuous over time. It does not follow from this social function of reward and punishment that all a society's economic gains from cooperation need to be distributed as rewards to virtue. The rewards that are most appropriate to the virtuous person are honor, respect, and admiration, not money, and the most appropriate punishments for the vicious are social contempt and ostracism. The amount of economic reward required for this educational function is only that amount necessary to properly honor people for learning and exercising their virtues. Similarly, the amount of punishment necessary is just that amount which will prevent people from learning to practice vices. Even though a system of reward and punishment is necessary to sustain a virtuous society, it does not follow that all the benefits and burdens of social cooperation must be distributed according to moral desert. There may be more total gains from cooperation than a society needs for educational incentives, so a society will need another scheme for distributing this surplus. The next chapter will canvas other theories of distributive justice that do not rely on a notion of desert.

Lastly, it is worth observing that there is something to the old saying that virtue is its own reward. The virtuous person is not motivated to be virtuous for the sake of a reward. A disciple of hedonism, who cultivates a life of pleasure and enjoyment, may end up leading a very pleasurable life, but a disciple of eudemonism, who cultivates a virtuous character, may end up leading a meaningful life, even if it is a life less enjoyable than that of the hedonist, or even if it is a life that is deeply unhappy in hedonistic terms.

2.5 Exercises

1. Summarize, in your own words, the Cultural-Relativity problem for thinking of justice as reward to virtue.
2. Summarize, in your own words, the Selective-Reward problem for accepting the distribution of rewards in a society as being fair.
3. Summarize, in your own words, the Proportionality problem for distributing rewards according to a member's contribution to a society.
4. Summarize, in your own words, why it may not be necessary for a society to distribute all its gains from cooperation as rewards to virtue.

CHAPTER 3

ACTING ON PRINCIPLE

ETHICAL REASONING CAN EVALUATE (1) THE CHARACTER OF THE DECI-sion-maker, (2) the motivation of the decision-maker, or (3) the consequences of a decision. In this chapter, we will focus on evaluating the motivations of decision-makers. Ethical decision-makers have good motives when they intend to act on good moral principles. However, it is perfectly possible for people with bad intentions to produce good consequences, and for the best of motivations to result in bad outcomes. Ethical reasoning that emphasizes motivations and intentions will praise actions done according to good principles, even if the actions have adverse consequences.

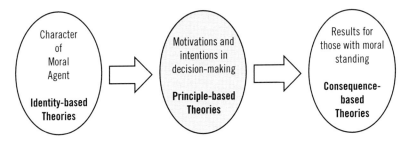

Figure 3.1: Categories of ethical theories. A person with a virtuous or vicious character is motivated by his or her principles to implement a decision that produces good or bad consequences for others.

Motivation by ethical principles often consists in the decision-maker fulfilling her ethical duties, regardless of the expected consequences of her decision. Duties are ethical obligations to act in certain ways. An ethical duty is an ethical obligation that overrides considerations of maximizing good consequences or of personal virtue. An ethical principle, in this pure sense, is a principle that should be acted on regardless of the consequences and regardless of whether a virtuous person would act in that way. It is always possible to derive a type of ethical principle from a character-based, or consequence-based ethical theory. The virtue-ethics rule of action, "Always do as a virtuous person would do," is a derivative ethical principle, not a basic ethical principle. It underlies a derivative, not a basic, duty. In ordinary English, confusingly, we refer to almost any ethical obligation as a duty. For example, we sometimes call the consequence-based ethical obligation to make everyone happy a "duty," and we sometimes say that the person who wishes to exemplify the virtue of honesty has a "duty" to tell the truth to other people. However, our primary interest will be in duties as basic principles that are independent of their role in creating happiness or exemplifying virtue.

We live our domestic lives within a tangled web of ethical duties. Some of these duties we openly discuss and agree to, such as keeping a promise or doing our share of the housework. Other duties we take for granted, such as duties to our family members or to our friends. Still other duties are legal ones, such as our duty to drive only on the correct side of the road or our duty not to steal from other people.

One view about our basic principles and duties is that our duties are the commands of God. Divine command theories of ethics hold that the commands of God create people's duties. Examples are the Ten Commandments given to Moses by the God of the Hebrews or the Golden Rule in the Christian New Testament. In what follows, though, we will look only at secular theories of principles, duties, and rights.

A second view is that our basic ethical duties are requirements of reason. Immanuel Kant thought that we have a duty not to do an action unless we can consistently claim that everyone can do that action without leading to the downfall of the very institutions within which the action makes sense. A third view is that we should simply list our basic duties according to our considered intuitions about the obligations that we have. These are our *prima facie* duties, duties that we have, but which stronger obligations can override.

A fourth view is that our ethical duties arise because other people have moral rights. A right is a justified claim by one person that other persons owe duties to her. For example, our basic liberties depend on our basic moral rights. Our freedom to lead our lives as we ourselves judge best depends on our moral right to lead our lives without the interference of other people. Our liberties impose duties on everyone else not to interfere with our lives. Often the source of an important moral duty is our obligation to respect the moral rights of another person. Moral rights and liberties, nevertheless, have limits. No one has a moral right to lead her life in such a way that she causes harm to other people. This is the so-called Harm Principle. The Harm Principle puts limits on the freedom of action of both individuals and organizations.

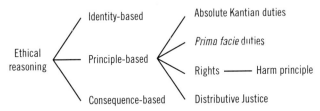

Figure 3.2: A conceptual map of four types of non-derivative, principle-based ethical reasoning.

A fifth view is that our duties arise from principles of justice. Distributive Justice is the requirement that we treat all persons fairly in the distribution of rights and duties. In this chapter, we will examine all these topics: duties, rights, the harm principle, and distributive justice.

3.1 DUTIES

The German philosopher Immanuel Kant (1724–1804) thought that only the motivation of the moral agent matters in the ethical evaluation of an action. He believed a person's action, which might appear to be right, was morally right if and only if (1) the action conformed to a person's duty and (2) the person performed the action because it was his or her duty to act that way. He gave the following example of a merchant who does not overcharge his customers.

> For example, it is in fact in accordance with duty that a dealer should not overcharge an inexperienced customer, and wherever there is much business the prudent merchant does not do so, having fixed a price for everyone, so that a child may buy of him as cheaply as any other. Thus the customer is honestly served. But this is far from sufficient to justify the belief that the merchant has behaved in this way from duty and principles of honesty. His own advantage required this behavior … (Kant 1959, 13)

Even though the shopkeeper does the right thing, which is not to overcharge the child, if he does it for the wrong reason, such as for the sake of his reputation, his action has no moral worth. Only if the shopkeeper does not overcharge the child because his motivation is his duty not to overcharge anyone is his action morally right.

Kant formulated an important theory of ethical duties that is still influential today. He distinguished between two types of principles: hypothetical and categorical imperatives. A **hypothetical imperative** is a strategic principle that will help someone get what he wants. A hypothetical imperative is a useful strategy that we can formulate in a conditional form. For example, the hypothetical imperative, "If you want people to trust you, then don't tell lies," is a useful strategy, but not a moral principle. A **categorical imperative**, on the other hand, is a moral principle of action that does not depend on anyone's wants or desires. A categorical imperative is an absolute duty, such as, "Don't tell lies," rather than a strategic principle.

Kant had a theory of absolute ethical duties. He thought that all absolute ethical duties stemmed from one main principle, which we now know as *the* Categorical Imperative, "Act only according to that maxim by which you can at the same time will that it should become a universal law" (Kant 1959, 39). Kant applies the Categorical Imperative to the case of a man who

> ... finds himself forced by need to borrow money. He well knows that he will not be able to repay it, but he also sees that nothing will be loaned him if he does not firmly promise to repay it at a certain time. (Kant 1959, 40)

According to Kant's Categorical Imperative, this man should notice that he is following a universal principle that says anyone who needs money can make promises he cannot keep. Then he should notice that it makes no sense for this principle to be a universal moral law.

> For the universality of a law which says that anyone who believes himself to be in need could promise what he pleased with the intention of not fulfilling it would make the promise itself and the end to be accomplished by it impossible; no one would believe what was promised to him but would only laugh at any such assertion as vain pretense. (Kant 1959, 40)

Because this principle, the moral law that people may make false promises to obtain loans, is self-defeating when we universalize it, the man has a duty not to act on the principle. That is, he has a duty not to make a false promise to obtain a loan. We cannot hold that people have no duty to repay loans, because if everyone had no duty to repay loans, then the entire financial, banking, and credit system would fail to function. But it is not relevant that this would make our lives worse; the point is that what would happen is that nobody would trust—or maybe even understand—a promise to repay. It would then be impossible to make a promise. Kant's theory tells us our ethical duties by asking us to first universalize what we think are our duties and to then see if this leads to some sort of contradiction. Kant makes failure of the universalizability of doing an action (such as breaking a promise) into an argument that there is an absolute duty never to do actions of that type (never to break promises). As we saw in the first chapter, universalizability is a requirement of moral principles if they are to be agreement-seeking.

The weakness of the Kantian view of duties is that it creates implausible ethical duties in extreme cases. Consider the philosophically famous case of the Truth-teller and the Axe-murderer. Kant's Categorical Imperative tells us that we have an absolute duty to tell the truth. The duty to lie whenever it is convenient to do so is not universalizable, because if everyone were to lie when convenient, then conversation, which depends on people being able to believe other people, would be impossible. Suppose that an Axe-murderer comes to the door of a house looking for his intended victim, who happens to be hiding in the attic. He asks the person who answers the door if his intended victim is in the house. According to Kant's theory, the person who answers the door has an absolute duty to be a Truth-teller and not lie to the Axe-murderer. However, Kant's duty-based theory just seems wrong in this extreme case. Utilitarian ethical reasoning works better; lying has much better consequences than does truth telling. Virtue-based ethical reasoning also works better in this case; the Truth-teller appears to suffer from the vices of being overly rigid and inflexible about her actions. Thus, Kant's Categorical Imperative is an instructive first pass at discovering what we have a duty not to do, but we must still weigh it against other sorts of ethical reasons to discover our overall duty.

A separate way to discover our ethical duties is to consult our considered moral judgments about moral obligations. This will result in a list of duties that, on the face of it, are morally binding on us, but which other, more powerful, obligations may override. **Absolute duties**, such as Kant's duty never to lie, are overriding obligations that people have no matter what happens. **Prima facie duties** are ethical obligations that people have, but which may yield to stronger obligations.

Scottish philosopher W.D. Ross (1877–1971) suggested a list of such *prima facie* duties (Ross & Stratton-Lake 2002, 42). He thought this list of duties met our considered intuitions about the ethical obligations that we have. His list included seven *prima facie* duties. The duty of beneficence is the duty to help others. The duty of fidelity is the duty to keep promises. The duty of gratitude is the duty to be thankful for benefits received from others and to reciprocate if possible. The duty of justice is the duty to treat others fairly and impartially. The duty of non-maleficence is the duty to avoid harming others as much as possible. The duty of reparation is the duty to compensate others if we harm them unavoidably. The duty of self-improvement is our duty to be the best that we can be.

Ross's list of *prima facie* duties could form the basis for making ethical decisions. *Prima facie* duties would provide us with a checklist of ethical considerations with which to examine problematic cases. Then in a case where *prima facie* duties conflict with one another, we would need to figure out our overall duty by seeing which *prima facie* duties are stronger. This is similar to the framework of ethical pluralism that we are using in this text.

In applying an ethical principle to a problematic case, it is often useful to ask, "What would happen if everyone were to follow this principle?" If the result were the breakdown of the social institutions that form the background of the whole situation, then we should conclude that we have at least a *prima facie* duty not to follow that principle. As Kant pointed out, if everyone were to lie whenever they wished, then discussion as we know it would become impossible. This is different from saying that everyone lying would make everyone unhappy. Causing unhappiness is a consequentialist worry that is of little importance, since it is unlikely that one of us telling a lie will suddenly cause everyone to start lying and being unhappy. Kant's point is a logical one, not a causal one. Contrary to Kant, though, it is a mistake to conclude that failure of universalizability leads to an absolute duty not to do some type of action. Absolute duties always have counterexamples, such as the case of the Truth-teller and the Axe-murderer. We are best to think of our moral duties as strong *prima facie* duties, but not as absolute duties that always override other applicable moral reasons.

3.1 Exercises

1. Formulate a definition for each of the following and repeat the definition aloud to help you remember it: (a) hypothetical imperative, (b) categorical imperative, (c) absolute duty, (d) *prima facie* duty.

2. Give an example, different from the shopkeeper example, of someone doing the morally right action with the wrong motives.
3. Describe a case that is a plausible counterexample to the absolute duty never to steal.

3.2 MORAL RIGHTS

Rights and duties relate in the following way. A **moral right** is a morally justified claim on others. The possession by one person of a moral right creates a duty for others to respect that right, a duty that correlates to that right. If Miguel has a right that Lori does Φ, then Lori has a **correlative duty** to do Φ that she owes to Miguel. It also follows that if Lori owes Miguel a duty to do Φ, then Miguel has a right that Lori do Φ.

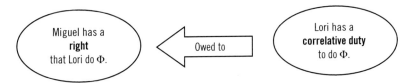

Figure 3.3: Miguel's right against Lori means that Lori has a correlative duty that she owes to Miguel.

The simplest type of right to understand is the sort of right created by a contract between two people. A contract creates a **specific right**, which is one whose correlative duty only falls on a determinate person or group. If Miguel loans $100 to Lori for 30 days, then the loan contract gives Miguel the right to claim $100 from Lori in 30 days and imposes a correlative duty on Lori to repay the $100 at that time. Only Miguel has this right, and only Lori has the correlative duty to repay Miguel. No other people besides Lori have the duty to repay Miguel. On the other hand, a **general right** is a right whose correlative duty falls on everyone. Like everyone, Miguel has a general right to his life. His right is a general one because everyone, not just Lori, has a correlative duty not to kill Miguel, a duty that everyone owes to him because his life is ethically so important.

Specific rights and duties may arise voluntarily when people make promises and enter into contracts. Specific rights and duties may also arise involuntarily through people's friendships, and family and community memberships.

We use the concept of a right in both ethics and law. Moral rights are rights that are justified by moral theories. Some moral rights are also legal rights, such as Miguel's right that Lori repay his loan or Miguel's right to life. **Legal rights** are legally enforceable rights. Some moral rights may not be legal rights because they are not legally enforceable under the laws of the applicable legal authority. For example, if Miguel promises to mow Lori's lawn on the weekend, Lori's moral right that Miguel do as he promised will not be the type of promise that Lori can enforce in the courts. It is often thought, in addition, that there are some legal rights that are not moral rights. Slave-owners had a legally enforceable general right to have runaway slaves returned to them; but those who were morally opposed to slavery thought that this was not a moral right, and imposed no moral duty on anyone to obey this law.

Rights can be either positive or negative. Someone's **positive right** imposes a duty on others to aid or assist the right-bearer in some way. Some examples are the right to disaster relief, the right to an education, the right to unemployment insurance payments, and, in many countries, the right to medical care. One problem with the notion of a positive right is deciding on whom the correlative duties fall. For example, if we accept that young people have the right to an education, then we must figure out who has the duty to satisfy this right. We would usually say that the positive right to an education imposes a duty on the state to provide an education to everyone, and that the state must find a fair way to spread the cost of supplying education to all its citizens.

Someone's **negative right** imposes a duty on everyone else not to interfere with the right holder's activities. It gives the right-bearer a liberty or freedom from the interference of others. Examples include the right to life, which protects each person by imposing a duty on everyone else not to kill him or her, and freedom of expression or freedom of association, which give people freedom from the interference of the government. The existence of negative moral rights is less controversial than the existence of positive rights, because it is easier to see who has the relevant correlative duties. People often suppose that negative rights, like the right to personal security, are on a stronger ethical footing than positive rights, like the right to medical care. However, it is worth noting that a negative right, such as the right to personal security, needs enforcement. The enforcement of the negative right to personal security imposes a duty on others to aid the person whose security is in jeopardy. The enforcement of negative rights thus creates positive rights. This again generates the problem of deciding who bears the correlative duties. We would usually say that the positive right to the enforcement of a negative right to personal security imposes a duty on the state and its government to protect its citizens. The state, then, must find a fair way to spread the cost of protecting personal security across all its citizens.

One of the main functions of negative moral rights is to stop the interests of society from dominating the interests of individuals. It might make everyone happier if the government were to silence a social critic with a prison sentence. The increased happiness of everyone else might outweigh the unhappiness of the imprisoned critic and thus be a happiness-maximizing reason for silencing her. But the critic's legal and moral right to freedom of speech will protect her individual interests from going unprotected in an overall happiness calculation. This conflict between the rights-based approach to ethical decisions and the consequence-based approach is a theme that runs throughout ethical decision-making.

Negative rights, freedoms, and liberties also protect people from interference by others, but rights and freedoms must have limits. As the saying goes, "Your freedom to swing your fists stops one inch from my nose." The Harm Principle that John Stuart Mill first formulated in his book, *On Liberty* (1859), sets these limits:

> ... the sole end for which mankind are warranted, individually or collectively, in interfering with the liberty of action of any of their number, is self-protection. That the only purpose for which power can be rightfully exercised over any member of a civilised community, against his will, is to prevent harm to others. His own good, either physical or moral, is not a sufficient warrant. (Mill 1859, 18)

The **Harm Principle** says that people (or the government) may interfere with other people's freedom, liberty, or the exercise of their rights only to prevent harm to others. For example, people have a negative right to freedom of movement. This freedom is not absolute or unlimited. Instead, freedom should have limits to prevent people from hurting others. Someone's freedom of movement does not extend to a moral right to drive her car on the wrong side of the road.

3.2 Exercises

1. Formulate a definition for each of the following and repeat the definition aloud to help you remember it: (a) moral right, (b) correlative duty, (c) specific right, (d) general right, (e) legal right, (f) positive right, (g) negative right, and (h) Mill's Harm Principle.

2. Give examples, different from the one in the text, of (a) a specific moral right, (b) a general moral right, (c) a positive moral right, (d) a negative moral right, and (e) a plausible application of the Harm Principle.
3. Explain, in your own words, why the existence of negative rights is, on the face of it, more plausible than the existence of positive rights. Why might negative rights require the existence of positive rights?

3.3 JUSTIFYING MORAL RIGHTS

Like the virtues, moral rights can have derivative justifications. A derivative justification of moral rights assigns moral rights based on an ethical theory that is not itself rights-based. One important example is the consequentialist justification of moral rights. Consequentialist reasoning can justify creating a system of derivative moral rights whenever that system would produce the greatest amount of moral value. For example, consider the Transplant Case. In the Transplant Case, five patients are each awaiting the heart, lung, or kidney needed to save their lives. These organs could all be available through the death of one innocent victim. A simple-minded consequentialism would justify such a transplant operation because the moral value of the five dying patients continuing to live would outweigh the moral value of the single innocent victim continuing to live. However, a more sophisticated form of consequentialism could argue that the anxiety and distrust created by allowing such practices would stop anyone ever going to the hospital. This would prevent hospitals from creating any moral value at all and so be self-defeating. Sophisticated consequentialist reasoning could assign all hospital patients a right to life, a right that temporary considerations of maximizing welfare do not override, because a right to life would maximize moral value overall.

One type of non-derivative justification for moral rights that is not based on consequentialist reasoning treats moral rights as natural rights. According to the doctrine of **natural rights**, rights-bearers have rights because they have certain natural features that are inherently valuable and thus needing protection by moral rights. One example of a set of natural rights is human rights. **Human rights** are moral rights where the relevant natural feature of the rights-bearer is being a member of the species *Homo sapiens*. Though being human is undoubtedly enough reason for having certain rights, it is implausible that membership in the species *Homo sapiens* is a necessary requirement for having any moral rights. If it were, then it would make no sense for animal rights activists to talk about chimpanzees (*Pan troglodytes*) having moral rights, or for anyone to talk of intelligent space aliens (of no determinable species) having moral rights, should they ever walk among us.

Ethicists have looked elsewhere for inherently valuable natural features that might explain possession of moral rights and have made two different suggestions. The **will theory** points to how the holder of a right has the power either to insist that others follow their correlative duties, or not to insist that they do, according to the right-holder's will on the matter. For example, Alice's promise to Ben that Alice will drive him to the airport creates a right: Ben's right that Alice give him that drive. According to the will theory, it is a right because Ben can choose whether to claim that right. At Ben's discretion, Ben can choose to claim his drive from Alice, in performance of her promise, or Ben can choose to relieve Alice of her promise and allow Alice not to drive him. In the limited matter of whether to give him that drive, Alice is morally subject to Ben's will.

One weakness of the will theory is that there are important moral rights the claiming of which is not at the discretion of the right-holder. Some rights are inalienable—that is, incapable of surrender—such as the right that others not enslave us. Contemporary society no longer allows people to sell themselves into slavery, even if they would choose to do so.

Another weakness of the will theory stems from the underlying natural feature that the will theory holds to be inherently valuable. This is the rights-bearer's ability to make competent, rational choices, a feature called "**moral agency.**" If potential rights-bearers did not have this ability, then there would be no point in using rights to secure their discretion over the duties of others. However, some persons, whom we think to have moral rights, do not have the ability to make autonomous choices. Small children, mentally incompetent adults, and people who are alive, but in a coma, have rights that we should respect, yet do not have the capacity for autonomous choice. From the point of view of attempts to extend moral standing to the non-human environment, autonomy is a feature of adult human beings not possessed by animals, plants, and ecosystems. So, the will theory is not compatible with the extension of moral rights to the non-human world.

The second theory of natural rights, the **interest theory**, holds that the inherently valuable natural feature that justifies possession of a moral right is what is importantly good for the right-holder. Here, the notion of an interest is not the idea of a person finding some feature of the world interesting and being curious about it. The ethical notion of having an interest is like the legal notion of an interest. For a person to have an interest in the performance of some action, the action must in some way benefit or harm, or be good for or bad for, that person. The interest theory of moral rights justifies a moral right because its possession is to the benefit or to the advantage of the right-holder.

The more commonly accepted forms of the interest theory of rights take interests to be subjective or psychological. In the psychological-interests approach to justifying natural rights, the natural feature that justifies a right is the mental benefits (e.g., pleasure, satisfied desire) that the rights-bearer will experience. One problem is determining which interests lead to rights and which do not. Someone's interest in continuing to live is an important interest that justifies a right to life. Someone's interest in having oatmeal for breakfast rather than cream of wheat is a trivial interest that does not justify a right to oatmeal. Somewhere we must draw a distinction between those interests that are urgent enough to justify rights, and those that are not. And it is not just trivial preferences that fail to create rights. Someone who seriously, intensely, for good reasons, wants that factory not to be built next door may not have the right to have its construction stopped. One criticism of the language of rights is the way rights proliferate: people enthusiastically assert their rights to all sorts of things. To sort out which interests lead to real rights and which do not, we need a criterion of importance for psychological interests. Not all psychological interests lead to rights. Psychological interests are features of human beings and (arguably) of other animals. The psychological-interests justification of moral rights opens the question of whether animals can have moral rights.

Another type of justification for the assignment of moral rights is justice-based. Distributive justice can justify a system of rights by arguing that this system is the best way to treat everyone fairly, or to treat everyone as equals. We will look at justice-based assignments of rights in the next two sections.

When we are applying the framework of duties and rights to making difficult decisions about how people should treat one another, we need to bear in mind questions about where those rights and duties come from. If people's rights appear to conflict, then we must look at the justifications of those rights in order to decide what to do. For example, the privacy rights of dementia patients in nursing homes may conflict with their rights to good care. Cognitively impaired patients are unable to communicate their own basic needs to their care-workers. Yet, putting a list of their needs on public view at their bedsides would apparently violate their rights to privacy. Their right to basic care and the right to privacy seem to be in conflict. Rights to care are interest-based rights while rights to privacy are will-based rights. The latter are justified because people should be able to choose for themselves who will have access to their personal information. Reflection on the different justifications of the two conflicting rights suggests the following potential resolution, though it is not one with which everyone may agree. Nursing home patients who are not cognitively impaired are capable of both communicating their own needs to care-workers and of deciding for themselves who should have access to their personal information. Posting a list of their needs in public view would be both unnecessary and a violation of their privacy rights. Cognitively impaired patients are neither able to communicate their own needs nor able to decide who should have access to their personal information. They do not have the psychological capacity necessary to justify a will-based right to privacy. Posting a list of their needs in public would not violate their right to privacy and would support their right to have their care needs met.

3.3 Exercises

1. Formulate a definition for each of the following and repeat the definition aloud to help you remember it: (a) natural rights, (b) human rights, (c) moral agency, (d) the will theory of moral rights, and (e) the interest theory of moral rights.
2. Give an example, different from the ones in the text, where utilitarian, overall happiness-maximizing considerations conflict with the existence of individual rights.
3. Give an example of a situation where a specific right fails to exist because of the lack of "informed consent." This is a situation where person-one tries to give person-two a specific right against himself, but where person-one is so extensively misinformed and lacking in information that person-two does not truly have a moral right against person-one.
4. Give examples, different from the one in the text, of the kinds of benefit-claims that some people call "rights," but which are implausible as true moral rights.

3.4 JUSTICE AND MORAL EQUALITY

Theories of justice, like theories of rights, are principle-based. They tell us to follow principles of fairness in how we treat others. Theories of justice take us into the realm of political philosophy. Political philosophy applies ethics to the basic structure of a country's legal system. Distributive justice is concerned with the fair distribution of rights and duties across those with moral agency and moral standing.

We treat people fairly by not favoring one person over another. For example, business firms treat customers fairly by giving them equal treatment. Justice requires that we treat people as moral equals, yet justice does not require that we treat everyone the same way. Instead, moral equality needs governments, business firms, and individuals not to treat people differently based on morally arbitrary features such as race, sex, age, religious preference, sexual orientation, and family background. At the most basic level, justice requires that we not favor one person over another based on such features. Paradigm examples of unjust societies include aristocratic societies, where positions in society go to those who are born to privileged parents, racist societies, where an overly large share of the benefits of cooperation go to people of one race and the burdens fall on people of another, and caste societies, where people are born into their positions in society and coerced into staying there for religious reasons.

On the other hand, treating people as equals requires that we recognize morally relevant differences between people. Society treats disabled people as equals by treating them differently when it gives them reserved, convenient parking spaces. Businesses reward workers who put in more effort. Justice is not as simple as treating everyone in the same way. Distributive justice may require that the rich pay income tax at a higher rate than do the poor. Interspecies justice will not give to animals the political rights that liberal democracies give to humans (rights to vote, to form political parties, to freedom of expression) because animals are incapable of exercising such political rights. Justice is not as simple as treating every entity with moral standing in the same way.

An example is Peter Singer's argument about the moral importance of animal welfare (Singer 1976). He begins from the basic moral principle that we should give equal consideration to the interests of all entities capable of having interests. From the perspective of ethical thinking, he says, we should not regard interests as of any less weight just because of whose interests they are. Moral equality is different from factual equality. Singer is not saying, for example, that all human beings are equally strong, smart, attractive, or the same in any other feature. He is saying, instead, that these features are not important from a moral point of view. To deny that the suffering of a being of non-human species matters, or to say that it matters less than the suffering of human beings, is what Singer calls "speciesism." Speciesism is the denial of equal moral concern based on species membership. Singer called it so to bring out the analogy to racism and sexism. The history of ethical development is in part the story of how people have recognized the moral standing of increasingly more of their fellow beings. The Ancient Greeks thought people who did not speak Greek were barbarians and thought it ethically permissible to enslave them. Until the nineteenth century, Europeans thought of Africans as potential slaves, and until the twentieth century governments did not give full legal standing to women.

Singer concluded that the interests of animals and people deserve equal consideration. By this, he does not mean to imply that the interests of animals and humans are the same. Humans have an interest in voting in elections, while pigs do not. We do not thwart the interests of animals by making no provision for them to vote in elections. No animal has the cognitive ability to make voting decisions, so it is meaningless to worry about satisfying an animal's interest in voting. According to Singer, we treat animals justly when we give the interests of animals the same consideration as the similar interests of humans.

In sum, an important part of applying ethics to problematic situations is figuring out how to treat everyone involved fairly in assigning rights and duties. Treating people fairly means treating them as moral equals. That is not to say that everyone is equal in their natural abilities or in their physical features. Nor is it to say that we must treat everyone in the same way. It is to say, however, that we should not treat them differently based on physical features that are morally arbitrary. It is also to say that we should treat them differently if we have morally relevant reasons for doing so. For example, it might well be that we should not discriminate in favor of people with good looks over people with ordinary looks, yet that we should discriminate in favor of people with poor physical mobility over people with ordinary mobility. The interesting question is always going to be which grounds morally justify discrimination and which do not.

3.4 Exercises

1. Describe a contentious example, one that people often disagree about, of a feature that supplies a *morally arbitrary* reason for discrimination.
2. Describe a contentious example of a feature that supplies a *morally relevant* reason for treating people differently.

3.5 DISTRIBUTIVE JUSTICE

Distributive justice involves treating people as moral equals when assigning property rights to economic goods and services. Different theories of distributive justice interpret the moral equality of persons differently. There are many theories of distributive justice and their interactions are complicated. What follows is only a brief introduction.

One approach to distributive justice understands moral equality as entailing no more than giving everyone an equal opportunity to compete for ownership of resources. A second approach, the libertarian view, understands moral equality as entailing equal respect for the natural rights of persons to acquire and exchange private property. A third approach, based on a utilitarian concern for human welfare, understands moral equality as entailing giving equal consideration to the welfare interests of every person. A fourth approach to distributive justice understands moral equality as involving equal respect for each person. This type of approach aims to distribute resources in a way that gives everyone a fair chance at personal happiness.

The first approach, equality of opportunity, says that a distribution is just if, and only if, it is the outcome of a process that allows people to compete for positions in society on the basis of morally relevant criteria such as ability or merit and not on the basis of morally arbitrary criteria such as race or gender.

However, there are several different conceptions of the nature of equality of opportunity. **Formal equality of opportunity** requires that there be no legal impediment to a person with certain talents competing for a position that requires those talents. People should get the position they deserve based on ability and past performance, and no organization should deny them these positions because of their race or gender. Business decisions often employ this conception of equality regarding employees, suppliers, and customers.

From the point of view of the moral equality of persons, the weakness of formal equality of opportunity is that morally irrelevant factors often determine people's talents. People's family background, their luck in the genetic lottery for intellectual ability, and their receipt of a good education often determine the talents with which they compete for positions. Factors that are arbitrary from a moral point of view often determine people's abilities, their willingness to exert an effort, and their productivity in society. Even though formal, legal considerations do not block them from the opportunity to obtain positions, their level of talent does. If morally arbitrary factors, such as the social class from which they come, determine their level of talent, then the distribution of positions will still be unjust.

Fair equality of opportunity tries to rectify this weakness of formal equality of opportunity by requiring that society make a special effort to provide a high-quality education to those who would otherwise receive a poor education. **Fair equality of opportunity** requires both that there be formal equality of opportunity and that society provide a uniform quality of education for all to give everyone a fair chance to acquire the skills needed to compete for social positions. Unfortunately, it is difficult for education to compensate for bad luck in the genetic lottery or for innate abilities. Fair equality is also not something that a single decision-maker can easily implement; it is something that only the whole society can create.

Feminists have pointed out that, even under conditions of fair equality of opportunity, there may still be structural inequality of opportunity. One example of the structural inequality of opportunity is that many positions in business and government are not really positions that people responsible for the care of small children can fill. Even if there are no legal impediments to a caregiver applying for the position, and even if these potential applicants are well trained and educated, the nature of the position and the demands it makes on the occupant's time may mean that the caregivers of small children cannot fill the position.

Structural equality of opportunity requires that organizations design positions in such a way that persons doing the necessary work of society, such as those responsible for the care of young children, can still fill those positions. Structural equality of opportunity is something that businesses can implement in the design of jobs and in the provision of services such as daycare.

Equality of opportunity in its various forms is not yet a theory of distributive justice. It removes various types of impediments to people applying for positions, but it does not say anything about what is the appropriate compensation for various positions. How should organizations distribute benefits to positions? The usual answer is that compensation should correspond to marginal productivity, or the marginal contribution that a person in this position makes to the firm. Arguably, the CEO makes a larger contribution to the profitability of a firm than does the janitor, and so her compensation should be correspondingly larger, though not ridiculously larger. The problem with using marginal productivity to determine compensation is that we cannot easily measure marginal productivity, and, when we can, it will often appear unfair as a gauge to compensation. In the modern world, goods and services are seldom the individual product of a solitary artisan but are instead the joint product of many people working together under conditions where it is not possible to disentangle who contributed what.

The second approach to distributive justice, **libertarianism**, holds that a distribution of rights and responsibilities is just if, and only if, it respects people's natural rights to self-ownership. Libertarian political theory tries to justify a system of unrestricted private property rights by tracking property rights back to a natural feature of human beings, their capacity for autonomous choice. The moral rights that protect autonomy are the negative rights of self-ownership. Self-owners are the opposite of slaves. Self-owners have the maximum possible liberty compatible with other people having the same. In particular, self-owners have the right to manage and sell their own labor. A libertarian argument for justifying a system of private property rights and a free market economy goes as follows: All people have a natural right of self-ownership to their own labor. When people labor on things that are un-owned, they come to own them, so long as they leave enough of the un-owned things for others. Therefore, people have a natural right to things acquired in this way. Their property rights in these things include the right to give, sell, or trade them with others. Therefore, people have a natural right to any property that they have acquired either by initial acquisition or by a freely made transfer from others. A libertarian system of property rights entails a minimally regulated, free enterprise economic system.

The premise in this argument about the initial acquisition of property comes from the influential writings of the seventeenth-century English philosopher John Locke (1632–1704). He formulated his theory in the following passage:

> Though the earth, and all inferior creatures, be common to all men, yet every man has a property in his own person: this no body has any right to but himself. The labour of his body, and the work of his hands, we may say, are properly his. Whatsoever then he removes out of the state that nature hath provided, and left it in, he hath mixed his labour with, and joined to it something that is his own, and thereby makes it his property. It being by him removed from the common state nature hath placed it in, it hath by this labour something annexed to it, that excludes the common right of other men: for this labour being the unquestionable property of the labourer, no man but he can have a right to what that is once joined to, at least where there is enough, and as good, left in common for others. (Locke 1689, Chapter 2, Section 27)

The notion of mixing self-owned labor with un-owned nature to create a privately owned economic good is a weak metaphor. Someone who pours his can of beer in the ocean and thereby mixes something he owns with something that is un-owned does not gain ownership of the ocean (Nozick 1974, 174–75).

The third approach to distributive justice is based in utilitarian thinking. Utilitarianism, which we will examine in detail in the next chapter, is the ethical theory that moral agents should bring about the best consequences judged in terms of the sorts of mental states that they bring about in others. Having positive mental states, like pleasure or preference satisfaction, is always in a person's interest. Utilitarianism implicitly treats people as moral equals because it considers everyone's interests equally. For example, it does not weight the interests of men higher than the interests of women when it comes to maximizing human welfare. Its implicit theory of equality is equal consideration of interests. **Equal consideration of interests** holds that a distribution is just if, and only if, it assigns the same weight to everyone's interests in the aggregation of interests for purposes of utilitarian maximization.

Equal consideration of interests, however, does not imply an equal distribution of resources. There is potential conflict between the maximizing concerns of direct utilitarianism and the fairness concerns of distributive justice. For the direct utilitarian, if an action that leads to the impoverishment of a minority happens to create the most aggregate happiness, then it is the action that a person should perform.

Another way to consider everyone's welfare interests equally is to argue that everyone should get an equal level of happiness or preference satisfaction. **Equality of welfare** holds that a distribution of property rights in resources is just if, and only if, it results in everyone having the same level of welfare. Equality of welfare is different from utilitarian justice because it says nothing about maximizing total welfare. Equal consideration of interests merely says that we should weight everyone's welfare interests equally in a utilitarian calculation. Equality of welfare makes the stronger claim that we should satisfy everyone's welfare interests to the same degree.

Neither equal consideration of welfare interests nor equality of welfare deals properly with the problem of expensive tastes. People with expensive tastes need more resources to give them the same level of welfare as people with inexpensive tastes. Champagne-lovers need more resources than beer-lovers to obtain the same level of enjoyment. It is unfair to give more resources to people with expensive tastes just to equally stimulate their jaded palates. Exquisite taste in wines is not a morally relevant factor in the distribution of resources in the way that requiring an expensive wheelchair is. People are responsible for developing their expensive tastes; people with mobility issues are not.

The fourth approach to distributive justice tries to avoid these problems by thinking of distributive justice as assigning rights to resources instead of assigning welfare to people. How people then use their fair share of resources would be up to them; if they want to buy champagne infrequently instead of buying beer frequently, then that is their business. The simplest version of equality of resources would just give everyone an equal share of income or an equal share of economic goods and services. Simple **equality of resources** holds that a distribution of property rights in resources is just if, and only if, it results in everyone having the same amount of resources.

Simple equality of resources just assigns everyone the same income to buy whatever resources they wish to have. It solves the expensive tastes problem because people with champagne tastes cannot demand more than an equal share of resources to satisfy their expensive tastes. It holds people responsible to form only preferences that are affordable with their fair share.

Unfortunately, strict equality of resources is vulnerable to the problem of leveling down to achieve equality. Strict equality of resources tells us that a distribution in which everyone gets the same share would be just, even if everyone would be better off in a society with an unequal distribution of resources. Nor does it hold people responsible for contributing to the production of goods and services; even those who choose to permanently camp on the beach with their surfboards will still receive their equal share of income.

In the most influential modern account of distributive justice, American philosopher John Rawls (1921–2002) proposed a way to avoid some of these problems. He set out his general conception of justice in his 1971 book, *A Theory of Justice*:

> All social primary goods—liberty and opportunity, income and wealth, and the bases of self-respect—are to be distributed equally unless an unequal distribution of any or all of these goods is to the advantage of the least favored. (Rawls 1971, 301)

He called his principle that an unequal distribution of rights to resources is fair so long as it betters the position of the least well-off the "difference principle." The **difference principle** says a distribution of rights and responsibilities is just if, and only if, everyone receives the same resources unless an unequal distribution results in the least well-off receiving more than in the equal distribution. Plainly, an unequal distribution of liberties or of opportunities to compete fairly for positions does nothing to help the least well-off, so the difference principle will give everyone the same basic rights and opportunities. However, allowing for some productive people to receive more than others as incentives to contribute will increase the total economic "pie" that is available to distribute to everyone. The resulting larger total wealth of society will allow for a larger distribution of wealth and income to the least well-off. The least well-off will receive more resources under the difference principle than they would have received under simple equality of resources. Thus, the difference-principle approach does not level everyone down to the same low level of well-being and resources.

Applying considerations of distributive justice to ethical problems is a complicated process. The different theories agree that societies should treat everyone equally, but they disagree on what is meant by equal treatment. To treat someone as a moral equal, should society give them equal opportunities, treat their self-ownership, property, and civic rights equally, consider their interests equally in making social policy, give them equal welfare, start them all off with equal resources, or distribute according to Rawls's difference principle, where the only grounds for any deviation from equality is to better the lot of the least well-off? In approaching a problematic situation, it is worth thinking about the situation from each of these perspectives. In simple cases, all the theories will give the same advice. In complex cases, it will be necessary to weigh the strengths of each theory's advice.

3.5 Exercises

1. Formulate a definition for each of the following and repeat the definition aloud to help you remember it: (a) formal equality of opportunity, (b) fair equality of opportunity, (c) structural equality of opportunity, (d) libertarianism, (e) equal consideration of interests, (f) equality of welfare, (g) equality of resources, and (h) Rawls's difference principle.
2. To get a job in the farm industry, a person must be able to heave around 40 kg. bags of grain. Many men, but few women, are strong enough to do this comfortably. Suppose the farm industry reduces the standard size of grain bags from 40 kg. to 25 kg. (88 lb. to 50 lb.). Would this be an example of formal, fair, or structural equality of opportunity in the agricultural job market? Why?
3. Suppose a policymaker is calculating what he should do by considering the amount of pleasure that would result from implementing policy A. He knows that implementing policy A would bring 30 units of pleasure to Mr. X, 50 units to Ms. Y, and 40 units to Ms. Z. He uses two different methods to calculate the aggregate amount of pleasure that would result. Each method uses a distinct way of weighting each individual's units of pleasure before adding them.

	Mr. X	Ms. Y	Ms. Z	Total
Method I	1 x 30 = 30	1 x 50 = 50	1 x 40 = 40	30+50+40=120
Method II	2 x 30 = 60	½ x 50 = 25	½ x 40 = 20	60+25+20=105

    a) Does method I respect equal consideration of interests? Why or why not?
    b) Does method II respect equal consideration of interests? Why or why not?

4. Suppose a policymaker is deciding between policy A and policy B. [N.B. In this question, he is deciding between policies, not methods of aggregation as in the last question.] He calculates the total amounts of pleasure that will result from each policy as follows:

	Mr. X	Ms. Y	Ms. Z	Total
Policy A	30	25	40	30+25+40=95
Policy B	25	25	25	25+25+25=75

    a) Which policy should a policymaker committed to equality of welfare choose? Why?
    b) Which policy would a utilitarian policymaker choose? Why?
    c) Which policy would level down welfare? Why?

5. Summarize the Expensive-Tastes problem for equality of welfare.
6. Summarize the Leveling-Down problem for simple equality of either welfare or resources.
7. A policymaker who focuses on distributing resources rather than welfare calculates the following distributions of money to Ron, Sal, and Tom.

	Ron	Sal	Tom	Total
D	$1100	$1100	$3000	$5200
E	$1000	$1000	$1000	$3000
F	$1200	$1300	$1500	$4000

a) Which distribution would simple equality of resources recommend? Why?
b) Which distribution would an economic version of utilitarianism recommend? Why?
c) Which distribution would Rawls's difference principle recommend? Why?

CHAPTER 4

CREATING GOOD CONSEQUENCES

ACCORDING TO IDENTITY-BASED ETHICAL THEORIES, A PERSON FACING an ethical decision should strive to be a good person. According to principle-based ethical theories, individuals should strive to do their moral duty, respect moral rights, and treat others fairly. According to the ethical theories that we shall examine in this chapter, a person should create moral value. Looking at a moral decision from these three perspectives will reveal all the ethical considerations that are relevant to the decision. It is helpful to think of these three approaches as a checklist that we can use in our decision-making so as not to miss any important ethical considerations.

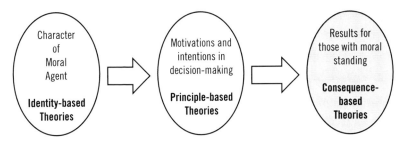

Figure 4.1: Categories of ethical theories. A person with a virtuous or vicious character is motivated by his or her principles to implement a decision that produces good or bad consequences for others.

Creating moral value, as an approach to ethics, suggests that decision-makers should bring about as much intrinsic moral value as possible and as little moral evil as possible. There are, however, different theories about the nature of moral value. Some theories are psychological and find moral value only in mental states such as pleasures and satisfied desires. These theories find moral evil in pain and frustration. Other theories find moral value in states of the world that are independent of psychological states. This chapter will examine several theories of moral value.

Self-interested people make decisions by looking at their options, calculating the consequences of each option, judging which options will contribute the most to their own welfare, and choosing those options. If each of us could neglect the interests of everyone else, and be morally concerned only with our own self-interest, then we would be ethical egoists. However, ethics is about cooperating with other people to everyone's advantage, and there are situations, such as the Prisoner's Dilemma, where rational decision-makers, concerned only with their own interests, cannot maximize their own advantage. This chapter will look briefly at a potential contractarian solution to this cooperation dilemma.

One theory that directly addresses the cooperation problem is utilitarianism, where the best decision is the one that causes the maximum amount of utility for all those whose interests it affects. Utility is a philosophical term of art that the originator of utilitarianism, English legal theorist Jeremy Bentham (1748–1832), defined as follows:

> By utility is meant that property in any object, whereby it tends to produce benefit, advantage, pleasure, good, or happiness, (all this in the present case comes to the same thing) or (what comes again to the same thing) to prevent the happening of mischief, pain, evil, or unhappiness to the party whose interest is considered.... (Bentham 1823, chap. I, par. 4)

Bentham took utility to be that property of an object that tends to produce welfare or happiness, which he took to be synonymous with pleasure. Bentham understood "utility" as another word for "usefulness." Modern-day economists and philosophers think of **utility** as an abstract measure of the welfare that people get from consuming something as a product or service. They think of it as an amount of pleasure or satisfaction, rather than as a property. Utilitarianism is a consequence-based ethical theory. So, to a utilitarian, a decision is the right one if, and only if,

1. it causes
2. the maximum
3. aggregate amount of
4. utility
5. for everyone affected.

Part (1) makes the decision procedure consequentialist. Part (4) makes it subjective or psychological. Part (3) says to add up or sum the utilities of everyone whose interests the decision will affect. Part (5) tells us not to forget any being with moral standing. Part (2) tells how to make the decision: Choose the action that will cause the greatest total utility.

Suppose that we have some way of measuring people's net utilities with a value in units of utiles, whatever those may be. In the table below, if Hal is an ethical egoist, then Hal will decide to do action A, because, by doing A, he will maximize his own welfare score at 30 utiles.

Hal's decision	Hal	Ira	Jan	Aggregate	Maximize?	Reasoning:
A	30	15	20	30+15+20=**65**	No	Ethical egoist
B	10	25	40	10+25+40=**75**	No	Pure altruist
C	25	20	35	25+20+35=**80**	Yes	Utilitarian

Table 4.1: A table of welfare scores (utility) for Hal's three options.

If Hal is a pure altruist (that is, a saintly person who maximizes positive mental states in others with no consideration of his own interests), then he will decide to do B because the joint welfare scores of the other two, Ira and Jan, is highest for action B (25 + 40 = 65). If Hal is a utilitarian, then he will decide to do C because C will cause the maximum, aggregated, welfare score for everyone, including himself. Defenders of ethical egoism claim that only the decision-maker has moral standing, defenders of saintly altruism claim that everyone but themselves has moral standing, and defenders of utilitarianism claim that everyone, including themselves, has moral standing. It is very important, when applying utilitarian considerations to an ethically problematic situation, to remember part (5) of the above formulation, which says to consider everyone who has an interest in the situation.

This chapter will look in more detail at the problems of measuring human welfare, and at the problems about distributive justice and respect for individual rights that occur when utilitarians add up welfare across many individuals. It will also look at the problems arising from the sheer complexity of the calculations that people must make in their ethical decision-making. One important solution to these problems is to apply the theory indirectly, at the level of policy formulation, rather than directly to each case. Indirect utilitarianism justifies the implementation of policies, such as the following of rules or the inculcation of virtues, rather than the performing of a net benefit calculation. The justification is that people will create maximum happiness by implementing these policies rather than becoming mired in a detailed calculation of costs and benefits every time they must make an ethical decision.

4.1 EGOISM AND CONTRACTARIANISM

Two types of theory stress the role of self-interest in ethics. **Psychological egoism** is the *scientific* theory that people always *do* act to maximize their self-interest. Since psychological egoism is a scientific theory, scientific experiments can, in principle, confirm or disconfirm it. It underlies the view of producer and consumer behavior in models of positive economics, and it is the view that the new field of behavioral economics calls into question. **Ethical egoism** is the *ethical* theory that people always *ought* to act to maximize their self-interest. Ethical egoism does not say that people always do act to maximize their self-interest; it says that people always should act to maximize their self-interest. Ethical egoism is a consequence-based ethical theory holding that only the self has moral standing. Decision-makers should consider only their own interests when they make ethical decisions.

It is important to note that ethical egoism is different from ethical relativism. The two theories work at distinct levels of abstraction. Ethical relativism is a higher-order metaethical theory about the nature of ethical reasoning. Ethical egoism is a first-order ethical theory about how people should behave. Ethical relativism says that right and wrong are relative to cultural membership, and many cultures are not ethical egoist. For example, the members of a monastic community might be dedicated to serving others. They might all believe in a life of saintly altruism for themselves that is quite the opposite of ethical egoism. Yet they are ethical relativists in the sense that they do not think that what is right and good for them is right for others. They are fine with the rest of the world being full of morally decent people who are not moral saints.

The biggest problem for purely self-interested egoists is that they have difficulty cooperating. We can begin to see this difficulty by examining the paradox of egoism. The **paradox of egoism** says that there exist states of affairs, which are in the self-interest of ethical egoists, but which these same ethical egoists cannot achieve because they ought always to act selfishly. Important relationships, like friendship, are in the self-interest of everyone, including ethical egoists. However, personal relationships such as friendship or marriage are not available to people who only act to maximize their own interests. Friendship requires that people sometimes put the interests of their friends ahead of their own. Extreme ethical egoists, however, ought to betray their friends whenever such betrayal is in their own interest. Thus, extreme ethical egoists cannot truly have friends and so cannot maximize good consequences for themselves. Extreme ethical egoism is self-defeating because extreme egoists cannot cooperate.

More generally, cooperation dilemmas arise in situations where two or more egoists can maximize their self-interest by cooperating but will be led to cheat to promote their own interests. Without the ability to cooperate, human beings would not flourish. English philosopher Thomas Hobbes (1588–1679) realized that extreme ethical egoists would always cheat on one another, and that life for a society of ethical egoists would be, in his words, "nasty, brutish, and short." He proposed that enlightened ethical egoists should set up a government with the coercive power to punish cheating. State punishment would then give cheating a lower payoff than cooperating and would thus make all the warring egoists better off.

We can see how this works if we develop the situation between Gog and Magog, the two hunters whose lack of cooperation showed the importance of ethics and morality. Suppose now that Gog and Magog both live in the same tribe, and that the tribe has a matriarch who enforces property rights, facilitates exchange, and makes perpetrators of harms compensate their victims. In particular, she will penalize any hunter who fights and steals with a penalty of 2 units of satisfaction. The new situation is shown in Figure 4.1 where any payoff that involves fighting is penalized by 2.

		Gog	
		Trade	Fight
Magog	Trade	2✓ ✓2	0✓ 3-2=1
	Fight	3-2=1 ✓0	1-2=-1 1-2=-1

Figure 4.1: A contractarian solution to the Prisoner's Dilemma. The matriarch of the tribe imposes a fine of 2 units on any hunter who steals or fights.

We can now see that Gog will trade no matter what Magog does, since $2 > 1$ and $0 > -1$. Similarly, Magog will also have a dominant strategy, which is to trade, and the two hunters will find equilibrium in the top left cell with 2 units of satisfaction each. This is an improvement over the Prisoner's Dilemma outcome in the lower right cell.

A **contractarian ethical theory** is a theory claiming that ethics consists in an enforced contract among ethical egoists designed to prevent dilemmas of cooperation. By accepting rules, egoists can avoid the war of all against all that Hobbes envisioned, and reap the benefits of cooperation. Nevertheless, egoists will endeavor to break the rules of the game whenever doing so is in their own interest. Ethical egoists are morally bound to pretend to cooperate, yet secretly cheat if they can get away with it, and psychological egoists will cheat if they can because it is their nature. Consequently, society will need legal enforcement of the rules of the game. There will need to be legal coercion of cheaters such as damage suits, fines, and prison time. This will require a large legal apparatus of police, lawyers, and judges. If cheating is widespread, then this legal apparatus will become overly expensive.

Internal enforcement would be less expensive. A society of people who were able to punish themselves for breaking the rules of the game would be economically more efficient than one where the tax system had to pay for a judicial system of punishment. People who were capable of self-punishment for rule-infractions—people who experienced feelings of guilt and shame when they took advantage of others—could cooperate more efficiently than could egoists who felt no remorse whenever they cheated. People who would regularly mete out informal punishment even at some cost to themselves—people who are outraged at cheating and indignant when they see advantage being taken—could also cooperate more efficiently than could egoists who were always calculating the costs and benefits to themselves of informally punishing others. People who had learned virtues of trust and trustworthiness could cooperate more efficiently than could people who had learned only to be selfish. In other words, a society of people who had internalized the rules of the game, learned a set of moral virtues, and acquired a set of moral emotions such as guilt, shame, indignation, and outrage, would be more productive than a society of people who only functioned through calculations of self-interest. Paradoxically, ethical egoists who committed themselves to other ethical theories, and thereby ceased to be ethical egoists, would, at least on average, find doing so in their long-term self-interest.

Despite all the foregoing problems with the pursuit of our own interests, self-interest should still be a consideration in ethical decision-making. For instance, the moral right of a person to act in his or her own best interest is protected by the important rights of self-ownership discussed in the last chapter. Ethical egoism is correct in identifying self-interest as an important part of moral decision-making, but it is wrong in suggesting that self-interest is the *only* concern. Rights of self-ownership are limited and must be balanced against other ethical concerns such as the demands of virtue and the importance of cooperation to create moral value. It is important to remember the dilemmas of ethical egoism, and to pay attention to other ethical considerations that often outweigh or override self-interest.

4.1 *Exercises*

1. Formulate a definition for each of the following and repeat the definition aloud to help you remember it: (a) psychological egoism, (b) ethical egoism, and (c) the paradox of egoism.
2. Explain the difference between ethical egoism and ethical relativism.
3. Give an example, different from the ones in the text, of a situation that involves the paradox of egoism.
4. Summarize the contractarian solution to the Prisoner's Dilemma.
5. Summarize a major difficulty for the contractarian solution to the dilemmas of cooperation.

4.2 EXPERIENCE-BASED UTILITARIANISM

Consequentialists have different opinions about the nature of moral value They differ in what they think utility is. Proponents of preference-based utilitarianism believe that utility consists in having preferences satisfied, where a preference is a person's choice among all the states of affairs that a person might want or desire. Economic, cost-benefit utilitarianism assumes that someone's willingness to pay for an option measures the intensity of their preference for that option. Proponents of experience-based utilitarianism believe, like Jeremy Bentham, that pleasure is the only thing that has moral value and that pain is the only moral evil.

Experiences are mental sensations of pleasure or pain, or feelings of enjoyment or suffering. They are action-guiding in that mostly people seek pleasure and avoid pain. For Bentham, pain and pleasure are also ethical. The first sentence of his important book, *An Introduction to the Principles of Morals and Legislation* (1789), gives the following advice:

> Nature has placed mankind under the governance of two sovereign masters, pain and pleasure. It is for them alone to point out what we ought to do, as well as to determine what we shall do. (Bentham 1823, chap. I, par. 1)

Pain and pleasure govern both what we actually do and what we ought to do. Experience-based utilitarianism is grounded in the ethical importance of feeling pleasure and avoiding pain. Because of the is-ought gap we cannot argue from the fact that people do avoid pain to the ethical value that people ought to avoid creating pain. However, the ethical value of avoiding pain is still an ethical intuition that most people share. Similarly, the fact that people seek pleasure does not entail that people should create pleasure, but the ethical value of pleasure is still a widely shared fundamental ethical intuition.

In the eighteenth century, in a society that assumed the interests of aristocrats were more important than those of everyone else, Bentham's utilitarianism was a radical doctrine. It treated everyone's interests as having equal importance in formulating public policy. Each was to count for one, and none was to count for more than one. Utilitarianism also promised a universal algorithm for making ethical decisions. If scientists could only find some way of measuring and comparing people's pleasures and pains, then utilitarianism suggested a recipe for ethical decision-making resembling the method of financial cost-benefit analysis: For each option, sum the pains and pleasures of everyone, and choose the option likely to cause the best balance of pleasure over pain.

Unfortunately, what works for individual, self-interested decision-makers is difficult to implement for decisions concerning more than one individual. First, single individuals can often compare one pleasure to another and determine which one is more intense, but scientists have not found a way to make this comparison between different people. Without a way of measuring degrees of pain and pleasure across individuals, it is impossible to sum and maximize net pleasure. Second, when individuals trade off their own pain for their own pleasure to maximize happiness within their own lives, issues of fairness do not arise. By contrast, when a utilitarian decision-maker trades off the pain of one person for the pleasure of a different person to maximize the summed total of happiness, issues of fairness become significant.

According to **experience-based utilitarianism**, the moral value of the consequences of a decision resides totally in the mental experiences that it brings about. An agent's decision brings about a state of affairs in the world, and this state of affairs causes pleasurable or painful experiences. This is the picture Bentham had in mind when he wrote of utility as the property of an object that tends to produce pain or pleasure.

Figure 4.2: Ethically valuable mental experiences brought about by a state of the world that standardly brings about such experiences.

One problem is that we can imagine creating any mental experience in a non-standard fashion. Sensations are purely internal to the mind and do not depend solely on what happens in the external world. For example, amputees frequently report pain in phantom limbs, even though the real limb is no longer there. We can design thought-experiments to suggest that sensations, feelings, and experiences are not the only things with ethical value. Philosophers test conceptual claims, such as the claim that pleasurable experience is all that is valuable, with thought experiments, just as scientists test empirical claims with scientific experiments. One such thought experiment is the Experience Machine, invented by American philosopher Robert Nozick (1938–2002):

Imagine a machine that could give you any experience (or sequence of experiences) you might desire. When connected to this experience machine, you have the experience of writing a great poem or bringing about world peace or loving someone and being loved in return. You can experience the felt pleasures of these things, how they feel "from the inside." You can program your experience for tomorrow, or this week, or this year, or even for the rest of your life. If your imagination is impoverished, you can use the library of suggestions extracted from biographies and enhanced by novelists and psychologists. You can live your fondest dreams "from the inside." Would you choose to do this for the rest of your life? If not, why not? (Nozick 1989, 104–05)

If we would not choose to hook ourselves up to the experience machine, then we do not really believe that only pleasurable experience has moral value. We do not value pleasurable experience if it comes about in a non-standard way. We also value the existence of the state of affairs that normally brings about each pleasurable experience.

Nozick's example suggests that what has ethical value for people is not only the experience, but also the state of affairs that brings about the experience. What one values is not only the mere feeling of writing a great poem, but also the fact that one really has written a great poem. In Bentham's terminology, what really matters to people is the existence of both the object that tends to bring about pleasure and the pleasure itself. Nozick's experience-machine example suggests that people want both an experience in their internal, mental world and a state of affairs in the external, real world.

4.2 Exercises

1. What is Bentham's theory of moral value?
2. Why is Bentham's theory of aggregating moral value democratic?
3. Why are the measurement and comparison problems more acute for utilitarianism than they are for ethical egoism?
4. Explain briefly the virtual reality objection to experience-based utilitarianism.
5. Give an example in which what people want is a state of affairs in the real external world, despite the fact that there will be no accompanying internal experience for them.

4.3 PREFERENCE-SATISFACTION UTILITARIANISM

Experience-based utilitarianism aims at producing pleasurable experiences directly. **Preference-based utilitarianism**, on the other hand, aims instead at producing actual states of affairs that people want. By giving people the states of affairs that they want, utilitarians hope thereby also to make them happy. Most people prefer the world to be such that their friends love them. They do not want the fake love of pretend friends; they want the real love of real friends. Utilitarians also think that people want the love of their friends because loving their friends and being loved in return will make them experience joy and happiness.

Contemporary utilitarianism, and the economic thinking that it underlies, has concentrated on satisfying people's preferences. Preference satisfaction depends on the external world being a certain way, and preference satisfaction requires that we change the external world to fit our preferences.

People always have many future states of affairs that they want to have come about. Because their resources are finite, they cannot satisfy all their wants and desires. They must choose the wants that they can afford to satisfy. For example, at the corner store, a child may want both a chocolate bar and a bottle of soda pop, but having only one dollar in her wallet, she must choose which of those treats she prefers. Figure 4.5 shows the stages of preference satisfaction. A person starts with a set of unrealized states of affairs, A to E, that he wants because he thinks they will bring him pleasure. Unfortunately, he can bring about only one of these states of affairs. Of the five states of affairs, he chooses D, which is the one that he thinks will cause him the most pleasurable experience. He prefers D and acts to bring about D. D satisfies his preference and gives him a certain mental experience. If he has chosen wisely, then his preferred D will bring him a more pleasurable experience than will any of his alternatives.

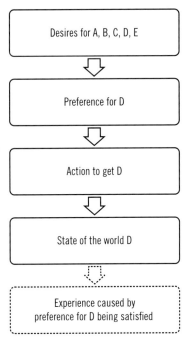

Figure 4.3: The stages of preference satisfaction.

The problem with using preference satisfaction to ground utilitarianism is that people do not always prefer wisely. We have all had the experience of wanting something, but finding that when we get it, it does not bring us any pleasure. For example, someone orders a slice of pepperoni pizza because she prefers it to the mushroom pizza and she anticipates the pleasure it will bring her. Unbeknownst to her the pepperoni has gone off, and the pizza tastes disgusting. We often do not have enough information to predict accurately the experience that we will have when our preference is satisfied. We get what we want, but it often does not make us happy.

To make matters worse, it turns out that we do not choose badly just because we lack information. Experiments in behavioral economics show that people systematically fail to predict the duration and intensity of experiences. Behavioral economists have noticed mechanisms that systematically cause people to misjudge the ability of their preferred states of affairs to bring them pleasure and pain. People form preferences regarding future experiences based on their memories of past experiences, when such memories are available. Memories of past experiences are systematically inaccurate. People's memories are subject to a tendency to neglect duration in the evaluation of past experiences and to remember, not the overall intensity of past experiences, but only their maximum intensity and their final intensity. For example, experimenters asked subjects to hold their hand in cold water for 60 seconds, which caused the subjects mild pain. Then they asked the same subjects to hold their hands in water for 90 seconds. For the first 60 seconds the water was at the same temperature as in the previous experiment, and for the last 30 seconds it was slightly warmer and less painful. The second treatment involved more pain than the first, because while both included 60 seconds of the same pain, the second contained an additional 30 seconds of milder pain. The experimenters then asked the subjects which treatment they would prefer repeated. Wise judges of how future states of affairs would cause them pain would choose the first treatment because it involved less overall pain. Yet many subjects preferred to repeat the second treatment. Their memories were unable to store the actual duration of the pain. So, they remembered the intensity of the pain in the final 30 seconds of the treatment better than they remembered their experience during the previous 60 seconds. They based their preference on their faulty memory of the experience, not on the actual experience itself. Contrary to what made sense to Bentham, and contrary to what made sense to the experimenters, subjects preferred pain of longer duration to pain of shorter duration, or more pain to less pain. Because people store memories of the experiences caused by past states of affairs in a biased way, they are liable to form preferences about future states of affairs in ways that systematically misjudge the psychological experiences that they will cause. People are bad at forecasting what will make them happy (Kahneman 2011, chap. 35; Gilbert 2006, chap. 10).

Thus, our actual preferences are sometimes a bad guide to what will bring us happiness. A better guide to happiness is to follow only the preferences that we would have if we had true and adequate information about how the resulting states of affairs would work out for us. The **informed preference theory of value** holds that a state of the world is morally valuable if it would satisfy the preferences that someone would have if she had had full information and were reasoning rationally. To return to our earlier example, we would not prefer the pepperoni pizza to the mushroom pizza if we had full information, that is, if we knew that the pepperoni had gone bad.

Sometimes our informed preferences are the same as our actual preferences. This happens when, in fact, we prefer the same state of the world that we would have preferred if we were fully informed. Sometimes, we are right about what will make us happy. Quite often, however, we are not, and then our informed preference for the mushroom pizza is different from our actual preference for the pepperoni pizza, which unbeknownst to us is rotten. What will promote our happiness is the mushroom pizza, the pizza we would have preferred had we known everything. The trouble is, our informed preference is not an actual preference that we have. Because it is a hypothetical preference and not an actual preference, we cannot measure its intensity. Therefore, we cannot measure and aggregate those informed preferences that people do not actually have in the way that utilitarianism requires. We can only do a net-benefit analysis over people's actual preferences, not over their hypothetical preferences.

On the one hand, philosophers are suspicious of using informed preferences in consequentialist calculations. World history is replete with examples of great harm done in the name of making people better or giving them what their rulers think they truly want instead of what they actually want. Using hypothetical, informed preferences can lead to a form of objective consequentialism that no longer worries about people's actual mental lives.

On the other hand, the informed preference theory of value can lead to sources of value that are not based in actual psychological states. We can imagine a case where no living person actually wants to preserve some beautiful, but isolated, wilderness area. So, preserving this wilderness satisfies no actual preferences, and brings about no pleasure for anyone. Yet, it might well be that if people were informed about this wilderness, perhaps by showing them newly taken satellite pictures, then people would prefer that this wilderness be preserved. There is now a sense in which the wilderness is valuable in a non-psychological sense; its preservation is valuable to possible, but non-actual, human beings according to the informed preference theory of value, even though its preservation creates no enjoyment or preference satisfaction for any actual human being. According to the informed preference theory, we can create valuable consequences that are not tied to any positively valued mental states of humans, or (for that matter) of animals.

An important moral that arises from this discussion is that in applying the general advice to create moral value by trying to give people what they want, we must be very careful in how we go about it. People's choices about which of their wants to satisfy may often cause unhappy, valueless, or even evil consequences. Yet, if we ignore what people say they want and try to give them what we think that they would want if they were rational and informed, then we risk disrespecting their personal autonomy, their right to choose for themselves. Creating value can easily come into conflict with respecting moral rights.

4.3 Exercises

1. What is the difference between experience-based utilitarianism and preference-based utilitarianism? What is an advantage of the latter theory?
2. What is the difference between actual preference-based utilitarianism and informed preference-based utilitarianism? What is the advantage of the latter theory?
3. People seem to be inaccurate in their predictions about the enjoyment they will experience when their future selves get what their present selves now want. Why is this a problem for preference-based utilitarianism?
4. Utilitarianism aggregates and maximizes moral value. To do this, it must be able to measure what it understands to be moral value. Explain the measurement problem for informed preference-based utilitarianism.

4.4 ECONOMIC UTILITARIANISM

One way of measuring the intensity of someone's preference for a commodity is to ask her how much money she is willing to pay for it. **Willingness-to-pay** as a measure of the intensity of a preference for a commodity is the greatest amount of money that someone would be willing to exchange for the economic good. It is important to see that what someone is willing to pay is not necessarily the market price. The market price for a commodity is set both by what people in general are willing to pay for an added item of that type and by what other people are willing to accept for giving up the item. When a market price exists for a commodity, no one will be willing to pay more for the commodity than the actual market price. Though most people would be willing to pay a great deal of money for a bottle of water in the middle of the desert, in the city they will not pay more for the same bottle than the asking price at the nearest corner-store.

Economic utilitarianism is a form of preference-satisfaction utilitarianism in which we measure the utility of a good or service to each person according to his or her willingness to pay for it. It becomes a utilitarian ethical theory when we add up the costs and benefits for each person affected by the alternatives, then add up each person's total to discover which alternative maximizes the grand total of financial net benefits for everyone, and then ethically justify our decision on the basis that our chosen alternative causes maximum aggregate net benefits. Economists use willingness-to-pay as a measure of utility when they do cost-benefit analyses. Economists are careful to distinguish when they are doing positive economics from when they are doing normative economics. **Positive economics** is a science that creates models describing the behavior of economic markets and participants in those markets. **Normative economics** uses economic science to ethically justify policy decisions. Normative economics is a moral approach to policy decisions, sometimes disguised as scientific fact. It tells decision-makers what policies they ought to implement based on an economic analysis of the policy alternatives.

Decision-makers use willingness-to-pay as a measure of utility when they do a cost-benefit analysis (CBA). A positive cost-benefit analysis is an economic technique that measures the financial costs and benefits of different policy options according to people's willingness to pay for them, calculates the total net benefits of each policy, and uses the results as a factual input to a policy decision. A normative cost-benefit analysis is a decision-making technique that measures the financial costs and benefits of different policy options according to people's willingness to pay for them, calculates the total net benefits of each policy, and uses the results to justify a policy decision ethically. It is important not to confuse these two interpretations of a CBA. What starts off as a factual inquiry can easily become an ethical decision-making criterion. When this happens, the results of the initial inquiry become an ethical decision without anyone noticing.

Table 4.2 shows the results of a simple CBA. For each person and each alternative, the analyst calculates the benefits and costs and subtracts to find the net benefit. For example, if Kira's benefit under alternative A is $450 and her cost is $300, then her net benefit will be $150 as shown in the top left cell of the table.

	Alternative A	Alternative B	Alternative C
Kira	$150	$150	$100
Mike	$200	$150	$100
Nadia	$250	$150	$500
Aggregate:	$600	$450	$700

Table 4.2: A CBA will sum the net benefits of each alternative and decide on the alternative with the highest total net benefits.

For each alternative, the bottom row shows the sum of the net benefits for all the three people. Alternative C maximizes net benefits and is the one that a normative CBA tells us to choose.

Clearly a positive CBA is on the "is" side of the "is-ought" gap, whereas a normative CBA is on the "ought" side. Proponents of normative CBA as an ethical decision-making technique can bridge this gap using an ethical theory as a premise. This ethical theory will be a form of utilitarian reasoning that uses people's willingness to pay (WTP) for outcomes to measure the intensity of their preferences for these outcomes. The following argument is logically invalid:

1. Alternative Q is the one that maximizes net benefits, as measured by WTP.
2. Therefore, we ought to implement alternative Q.

The ethical ("ought") conclusion does not follow from the factual ("is") premise. However, if we supplement the argument with a utilitarian ethical premise, then it becomes logically valid. The following argument is valid—that is, the conclusion follows from the premises:

0. Whatever alternative causes maximum net benefits, as measured by WTP, is the one we ought to implement.
1. Alternative Q is the one that maximizes net benefits, as measured by WTP.
2. Therefore, we ought to implement alternative Q.

The argument is logically valid, but whether it is a sound argument depends on whether the ethical premise is true or not. If the ethical premise is false, then, despite the argument's logical validity, the argument lends no support to its ethical conclusion, the decision to implement alternative Q. The missing premise that we added to the above argument, clause 0, is a statement of economic utilitarianism.

One problem with normative cost-benefit analyses is that decision-makers often apply them only in a limited context. For example, a cost-benefit analysis done for a firm may limit itself to just the interests of owners and employees. However, economic utilitarianism should imply that all people have moral standing. So, any decision-maker using a normative cost-benefit analysis should be careful to consider the costs and benefits for all parties the decision affects.

Another problem with normative cost-benefit analyses is that ability-to-pay affects willingness-to-pay, which is economic utilitarianism's measure of utility. If a billionaire and a worker are both at an auction bidding on a rare coin, the price that the billionaire would be willing to pay will be far higher than the price that the worker could pay. This is not a sign that the billionaire wants the rare coin more intensely than the worker does, or that possessing the coin would make the billionaire happier than it would the worker. All it means is that the billionaire has more money than the worker has. We could only use willingness-to-pay to compare preference intensities among people with the same income and wealth. Since income and wealth vary widely across the population, willingness-to-pay will be a faulty measure of preference intensity. Furthermore, if we do use willingness-to-pay as a measure of preference intensity, we will end up weighting the preferences of well-off people more highly than we weight the interests of low-income people. A billionaire with the same preference intensity as a worker will nonetheless be willing to pay (because able to pay) more to satisfy that preference than will the worker. This is unfair and contrary to a major attraction of utilitarianism, its equal consideration of interests, as in Bentham's slogan, "Each to count for one, and none to count for more than one."

Against the background of the market societies in which all of us live, it is easy to think that moral value is always the same as financial value. Sometimes it is, but certainly not always. When we are applying the advice to create moral value, we should always reflect critically on the degree to which creating financial value actually does create moral value. And, as always, we should be prepared to balance the advice to create financial value with considerations of what is virtuous, what is caring, what is fair, and what respects people's rights.

4.4 Exercises

1. Formulate a definition for each of the following and repeat the definition aloud to help you remember it: (a) willingness-to-pay, (b) economic utilitarianism, (c) positive economics, and (d) normative economics.
2. (a) What is the relationship between someone's willingness to pay for a commodity and the market price of the commodity? (b) Why does this make it difficult for an economist to measure the intensity of the person's preference for the commodity?
3. With reference to Table 4.2, what would someone who was committed to the moral equality of persons and to an egalitarian theory of distributive justice say about the choice of Alternative C by a proponent of normative cost-benefit analysis?
4. Explain the Ability-to-Pay problem for using willingness-to-pay as a measure of the intensity of preferences.

4.5 INDIRECT UTILITARIANISM

Some of the worst difficulties with utilitarianism as an ethical theory arise because of the way that it maximizes total welfare by adding up, or aggregating, everyone's interests without regard to what happens to the individual human beings over whom it is summing. The requirement to aggregate interests is implicit in Bentham's description of the nature of a community:

> The community is a fictitious body, composed of the individual persons who are considered as constituting as it were its members. The interest of the community then is, what?—the sum of the interests of the several members who compose it. (Bentham 1823, chap. I, par. 5)

Aggregating everyone's interests can lead to the violation of individual human rights, unfair distributions of welfare, and demands for people to behave in utility maximizing ways that are contrary to becoming a virtuous person.

A stock example of the problems that aggregation creates for utilitarianism is the case of the transplant surgeon. In the transplant ward of a hospital, two patients each need a kidney, two patients each need a lung, and one patient needs a heart. All five patients will die if they do not receive these transplants. Another patient arrives at the hospital with a broken leg, but also with two healthy kidneys, two healthy lungs, and a healthy heart. The surgeon could save the five dying patients by removing the healthy organs from the one with the broken leg. She would thus satisfy the preferences to continue living of five people by frustrating the preference to live of only one person. Utilitarianism would approve this trade-off, but other ethical approaches would not. According to the rights approach, the surgeon would be violating the sixth patient's right to life. According to the justice approach, she would be treating the sixth patient unfairly, imposing a giant burden on him for the morally arbitrary reason that he happened to break his leg at the wrong time and place. According to the care ethics approach, the surgeon is undermining the caring and trusting relationship that should exist between doctor and patient. According to the virtue approach, the surgeon is murderous and callous. Because it aggregates welfare without concern for the individual, utilitarian reasoning can violate our most basic moral intuitions as summarized in other ethical approaches.

Utilitarianism suffers from two further difficulties when considered as an ethical decision-making technique. First, applying utilitarian reasoning to every case is cumbersome, time-consuming, and expensive. This is clear from the technique of using cost-benefit analyses to perform environmental impact studies. Such decisions are not simple ones, need a great deal of staff time, and are expensive, especially when done by outside consultants. Utilitarian reasoning is similarly demanding for individuals. Each time she makes an ethical decision, an individual must (a) figure out who each of her alternatives will affect, (b) predict the net welfare change of each affected person, (c) decide on probabilities of outcomes, (d) calculate the aggregate net welfare for each alternative, and finally (e) choose the alternative that maximizes net welfare. This very complicated deliberation will be hugely demanding on the cognitive abilities of decision-makers. Because "ought" requires "can," if a direct utilitarian decision-making procedure is overly demanding on decision-makers, then it cannot be morally required.

Secondly, utilitarian decision-making is likely to neglect tiny consequences that, though insignificant by themselves, accumulate into important welfare effects. A stock example is the lawn-crossing problem. One person walking on the grass in a park will have no significant effect on the grass, or on anyone's enjoyment of the lawn. The growth of grass will soon fix any damage. Each person, when reasoning in a direct utilitarian way about what to do, will legitimately decide to walk on the grass. Nevertheless, many people walking on the grass over an extended time will destroy the grass and ruin everyone's enjoyment of the lawn. It is important to see here that these are not merely multiplication effects. If one person's walk causes literally *no* harm to the lawn, then 100 people's walk does not cause 100 times that much. One hundred times zero is still zero. They are effects brought about by the crossing of some non-linear tipping-point or threshold for harm. Another example is the effect of driving gas-guzzling automobiles on climate change. One person driving a gas-guzzler will have no effect on the climate, but millions of people doing so for years on end will have catastrophic consequences.

A solution to all these problems is to say that we should not apply utilitarian reasoning to individual decisions and acts, but instead should use utilitarian reasoning to justify rules and policies, that if followed, would maximize overall happiness. For example, if people follow the rule, "Keep off the grass," then everyone will enjoy the lawn more than they would if people must decide whether to cross on every individual occasion.

We can extend this line of thought further to reduce some of the rights, justice, and character-based difficulties brought about by utilitarian reasoning's commitment to aggregation. Applying utilitarian reasoning indirectly can justify a whole suite of policies, including rules, human rights, principles of justice, and character education provided that, when implemented, they will maximize overall utility. **Direct utilitarianism** treats utilitarian reasoning as a decision procedure and judges each case according to a calculation of the utilities it causes. **Indirect utilitarianism** treats utilitarian reasoning not as a decision procedure, but as a justification procedure. It advocates obedience to rules, respect for rights, inculcation of virtues, and the creation of whatever policies are necessary to maximize aggregate utility. The system is morally justified because the entire system maximizes utility.

Employing utilitarianism indirectly may avoid the difficulty of the transplant surgeon case. Indirect utilitarian reasoning would justify assigning hospital patients a right to life, as well as educating surgeons in the Hippocratic Oath, "First, do no harm." These policies are morally justified because otherwise no one would use hospitals out of fear that a utilitarian calculation might cost them their lives. Indirect utilitarianism recommends that, instead of using utilitarian reasoning to decide what to do in each case, we should use utilitarian reasoning to determine a system of policies, rights, mechanisms of distributive justice, and methods of instilling virtue.

Applying utilitarianism indirectly offers a way of adjudicating between the competing advice offered by different ethical approaches. But it only works if we have already decided on which version of utilitarianism—experience-based, preference-based, economics-based, or informed preference-based—is the one that always works, and which we will use to do our adjudicating. However, without begging the question, we cannot use any one version of utilitarianism to adjudicate between all versions of utilitarianism. If we use, for example, experience-based utilitarianism to tell us the variety of utilitarianism on which to base indirect utilitarian reasoning, then the answer is obvious, but the overall argument is absurd. Each type of utilitarian reasoning has its strengths and weaknesses, and we need to look further at how to balance them against one another. This suggests that we need another way, besides applying utilitarianism indirectly, to balance utilitarian reasons against moral reasons stemming from the virtue ethics and rights and justice approaches.

4.5 Exercises

1. Distinguish between direct utilitarianism and indirect utilitarianism.
2. How would direct and indirect utilitarianism each apply to human actions that collectively bring about harmful climate change?
3. Why is it usually easier to apply indirect utilitarianism to an ethical problem than it is to apply direct utilitarianism to the same problem?
4. Suppose, for the sake of argument, that there existed one society, A, with some contented slaves, that was happier overall than another society, B, with only free people. How would direct utilitarianism and indirect utilitarianism evaluate these two societies?

4.6 TELEOLOGICAL AND HOLISTIC ETHICS

Up to now, we have been examining theories of moral value where the created value is in some way psychological. We have looked at advice to create the maximum amount of pleasure, the maximum amount of preference satisfaction, the maximum number of informed preferences that are satisfied, and the suggestion that the best way to meet any of these psychological goals is to work on them indirectly. In each case, the morally valuable thing that the theory recommends creating is a psychological state. However, it is possible to have theories that recommend creating non-psychological moral value, either instead of, or as well as, psychological moral value. We will look at two of these.

Teleological theories of moral value claim that much of the activity in the natural world is goal oriented. Some of this is psychological, as when humans set goals for themselves, and some of this is non-psychological, as when we talk of a tree flourishing and striving to reproduce. This latter sort of theory recommends that we should do what is good for all living things, not just those creatures that have mental states.

Holistic theories locate moral value in the complex organization of elements of both the human and the non-human world. Creating and sustaining institutions such as governments, cities, business corporations, and universities is morally valuable, as is protecting the organization of living things into natural ecosystems. The moral value of the organized whole is not reducible to the individual moral value of its parts.

A teleological conceptual framework understands everything in terms of its natural purpose, its potential, or its function. The term "teleological" comes from the Ancient Greek word *telos* meaning "function" or "purpose." To people living in a world of tools and machines designed to fulfill the (mental) purposes of human beings, the teleological conceptual framework is normal and everyday. However, the teleological conceptual framework at once suggests an ethic. What is *good for* a plant is whatever enables it to flourish and fulfill its potential or natural purpose. It is easy to take this non-moral conception of the good and moralize it. For example, people sometimes argue that because Darwinian evolutionary theory is about the survival of the fittest, the natural purpose of a living thing is to survive. Therefore, moral agents ought to promote the flourishing of all living things.

The role of flourishing in teleological consequentialism is quite different from its role in virtue ethics. In teleological consequentialism, a moral agent should cause good consequences, where good consequences are those that are good for the flourishing of morally considerable beneficiaries. We picture this in Figure 4.4.

In virtue ethics, a moral agent strives to be a flourishing person. To flourish,

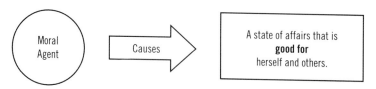

Figure 4.4: Teleological Consequentialism. Agent causes what is good for themselves and others.

needs a good character. Having a good character means having good character traits. Possessing good character traits means having strong virtues. In virtue ethics, the virtues are morally required not because they cause people to flourish, but because possessing virtues is part of what it means to flourish. We illustrate this pictorially in Figure 4.5.

A plausible theory about the development of human intelligence is that it evolved, not to aid our interaction with the natural world, but to aid our

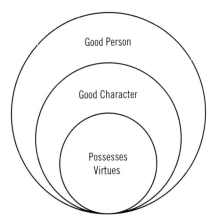

Figure 4.5: Virtue Ethics. Good agent has a good character because she is virtuous.

interaction with other people. To interact either cooperatively or exploitatively with people in large groups, humans needed to understand the purposes and plans of other humans. Thus, when human intelligence tried to understand the non-human world it was natural for it to start by looking for the purposes of everything. For example, it is natural to understand the heart as an organ whose purpose is to pump blood. This sort of understanding was useful, but it did not take medical doctors far in their quest to treat heart disease.

One attraction of the teleological approach to moral value is that teleological reasoning allows the extension of moral standing to entities that have natural purposes. It allows moral consideration of non-human and even non-animal entities that do not feel pain and pleasure, do not have preferences, and cannot make rational, autonomous decisions about what they want to do. Despite this attraction, the teleological approach to value has weaknesses. For one, teleological reasoning can confuse the non-moral sense of something being good for an entity with the moral sense of some state of affairs being a good one. Even if it is good for the virus causing COVID-19, severe acute respiratory syndrome coronavirus 2 or SARS-CoV-2, to find a new host in the non-moral sense, it does not follow that it is good in the moral sense for people to pass on SARS-CoV-2 to others. Additionally, the teleological approach to biology is now out of date. Teleological explanations have given way to evolutionary and molecular biology explanations. Nonetheless, it is no longer the basis of scientific understanding.

Holistic theories of moral value say that agents ought to contribute to the betterment of the community-as-a-whole. Here the community-as-a-whole is something other than the mere sum of its individual parts. If the good of the community were the aggregate good of all the members of the community, then common good theories would just be versions of utilitarianism. It is a familiar idea that a whole may be different from its parts or even the sum of its parts. For example, the individual members of a community, the people who are its parts, all have psychological states, whereas the community itself does not have psychological states. The common good, the good of the community-as-a-whole, is distinct from the total utility of the community. Even though achieving the common good may benefit individuals, this is not its aim. In a holistic theory, the good of the community can trump any and all individual goods or aggregations thereof.

Working to increase a country's Gross Domestic Product (GDP) would count as working to increase the sum of the individual goods of all the country's citizens. Working for the common good of the citizens of a country consists in helping the country's political institutions and systems of social cooperation to function in a healthy way. This may benefit citizens, but it will do so in a different way from just maximizing the sum of their individual goods. We are familiar with other examples where the interests of entities are not reducible to their component individuals. Business corporations are characterized by a high degree of organizational structure that enables them to exist as stable entities in a market economy, even though their workers, managers, and owners change continually. We can understand how some government policy might be good for corporations by protecting their stable existences and helping them to flourish. The same is true of condominium corporations, municipalities, provinces, states, and nations, which also exist as stable, complex, highly organized entities.

Structurally, the community-good approach is compatible with the extension of moral standing to ecosystems, if we conceive of them as living communities. Such a non-anthropocentric extension would be a holistic, as opposed to an individualistic, conception of the good. For example, American environmentalist Aldo Leopold (1887–1948) proposed that ecosystems should also have moral standing. He wrote that "A thing is right when it tends to preserve the integrity, stability, and beauty of the biotic community. It is wrong when it tends otherwise" (1949, 262). Leopold's definition of his land ethic has been very influential in the development of non-anthropocentric ethical theories. "The land ethic simply enlarges the boundaries of the community to include soils, waters, plants, and animals, or collectively: the land" (Leopold 1949, 239).

One problem for the community-good approach is that its central notion may seem mysterious. Increasing the intrinsic good for individual members of a community has an obvious appeal; but what could be the value to anyone of a so-called good that does not benefit individuals? For this reason, the incentives of community members may differ from their moral obligations. Community members may be happy to accept any benefits of community membership but be reluctant to contribute to conserving and bettering the community, its institutions, and its environment, when this is unrelated to good results for them or other community members. Even if they value these community goods, they may be tempted to free-ride on the contributions of others, knowing that the contributions of others will keep the community healthy.

Another problem is that the common good approach is prone to accept violations of rights, and reductions in the welfare of individuals. For example, in the nineteenth century, loyal subjects died for the good of the British Empire. In the twentieth century, the fascists in Nazi Germany murdered millions of people for what they saw as the health and glory of the so-called "Third Reich." The common good approach does not have the intellectual resources necessary to justify protecting the rights of individual members of the community. Similar conflicts can arise between holistic, ecological ethical theories and individualistic, animal rights theories.

Examining the informed preference, the teleological, and the common good approaches to a consequentialist ethic reminds us that in applying ethics, we should consider the potential importance of creating non-psychological value. Some consequences may be intrinsically valuable in ways that go beyond their usefulness in creating pleasure, satisfying preferences, or creating economic value. Sometimes the intrinsic value of some consequence, such as preserving a wilderness, protecting a work of art, or enabling a tree to flourish, may come into conflict with, say, maximizing economic value. For example, consider a decision to preserve a wilderness area that is based on the moral reason created by these non-psychological sources of value. This moral reason may sometimes be overridden by another reason, for instance, that such a decision would lead to a violation of the rights of an indigenous community. But often the non-psychological moral reason may not conflict at all, or it may conflict only slightly. For example, suppose preserving a wilderness area would cost a small number of tax dollars that could have been used to slightly increase the welfare of a few taxpayers. Now the non-psychological wilderness-preserving reason must be weighed against the, ultimately psychological, taxpayer-based reason, and the best overall decision is less obvious.

4.6 Exercises

1. What is the difference between a psychological and a non-psychological theory of moral value?
2. Briefly explain how flourishing plays a different role in teleological consequentialism from the role it plays in virtue ethics.
3. How has contemporary science weakened the credibility of teleological moral reasoning?
4. Briefly explain how the good of the community-as-a-whole differs from the sum of the goods of the members of the community.
5. A philosophical proponent of animal rights once described the Land Ethic as "environmental fascism" (Regan 1983, 361–62). What do you think this means?

CHAPTER 5

WHO IS RESPONSIBLE? WHO COUNTS?

TO SAY THAT SOMEONE IS MORALLY ACCOUNTABLE FOR THE OUTCOME of her decision is to make a value judgment. It is a value judgment because it says that we should either praise or blame her for her decision, that we should either admire or scorn her for her character, or that we should either reward or punish her for the result of her decision. These are not factual judgments; they are ethical judgments.

To say, however, that someone is causally responsible for an outcome is to make a factual judgment. It is a factual judgment because it says that some action that he intended to perform, and then did perform, caused the outcome to happen. It is a factual judgment because to see if it is true, we need to investigate his mental state, his physical behavior, and the existence of a causal connection between his action and the outcome.

Because of the "is-ought" gap, then, to say that someone is causally responsible for an outcome is not to say that he is morally accountable for the outcome. His causal responsibility is a factual judgment, while his moral accountability is a value judgment. To move from causal responsibility to moral accountability, we need an added premise taken from ethical theory. One ethical view that connects causal responsibility and moral accountability is the idea of retributive justice; society ought to punish a person for an action if (1) his action causes harm to others, and if (2) he intended his action to cause this harm. In the criminal law, there are two similar requirements for a person to be guilty of a crime: (1) he was the cause of the harm (in legal Latin, *actus reus*—the "guilty act") and (2) he understood that he was causing harm and that this was wrong (*mens rea*—the "guilty mind"). To secure a conviction and have the defendant punished, the prosecution must prove that both conditions were present in the alleged crime.

The retributive-justice-plus-causal-responsibility model of moral responsibility is prevalent in our culture. People often defend their actions by arguing either that they did not intend a bad result or that we cannot prove that their actions caused the bad result, and then consider it unfair if we blame them for their actions. For example, suppose Amy, a manager, argues for outsourcing production to a country with weaker safety standards than her own, that her firm's cost-cutting committee accepts her recommendation, and that the off-shore factory later collapses with multiple casualties. Amy might easily argue that she has no responsibility for the factory collapse because she only intended to increase company profits, or because her role in the decision was so small that it did not cause the unsafe building to collapse.

Nevertheless, retributive justice is not the only approach to ethics or to moral accountability. Virtue ethics would hold Amy accountable for the character traits that she displayed in her actions. Was she either stupid or willfully ignorant in not knowing of the safety risks in overseas factories? Knowing these risks, was she careless or reckless in recommending offshore production? Ethical theories that appraise the motives of decision-makers might also hold Amy accountable. Did she think only of her yearly bonus, and did greed motivate her in her recommendation? Did she disregard principles of respect for human rights or of the fair distribution of risk? There are reasons for holding people morally accountable other than the combination of retributive justice and causal responsibility.

In addition, the notion of causal responsibility is not as precise as we might initially assume. The determination of causality is a scientific operation; science is precise and non-subjective, and so we might expect determination of causal responsibility to be precise and non-subjective as well. Yet, when we examine the determination of causal responsibility in more detail, we find that the notion of one condition being the cause of another is not as simple as we would hope. In this chapter, we will look at the scientific notion of causal responsibility in some detail and examine some of the difficulties that arise in deciding causal responsibility.

Philosophers have worried extensively over whether a freely made decision is even possible. This is the metaphysical problem of free will. Science appears to show that every event in the world is causally determined. All decisions made by agents are events in the world. Therefore, all decisions are causally determined. If a decision is causally determined, then it is not a freely made decision. Therefore, no decision is a freely made decision, and people are never morally responsible for their actions. Solving this metaphysical problem is far beyond the scope of this discussion. We will assume that, in the absence of external interference, most of our decisions are freely made. We are normally autonomous, both personally and morally. We will, however, look at the problem of what constitutes an interference with an agent's personal or moral autonomy.

5.1 MORAL AGENCY

What sort of entities have moral autonomy and are thus morally accountable for their decisions? A precondition for being morally accountable is being a moral agent. A **moral agent** is an entity to which we are prepared to assign praise or blame, which can respond to moral reasons, and which we are prepared to hold morally accountable. To have moral agency, an entity needs certain capacities. These include moral sensitivity, responsiveness to ethical reasons, and decision-making abilities. Any interference with an agent's moral autonomy can be an interference with their moral agency because it interferes with their ability to respond to ethical reasons and to make ethical decisions based on those reasons. We know that most adult human beings can be morally autonomous, but what about, for example, business corporations? Is a business corporation a moral agent?

To be sensitive to the existence of moral issues, an ideal moral agent needs a range of emotional capacities. The agent needs empathy, the ability to understand the feelings of a broad range of others. The agent also needs sympathy for others, which is the capacity to have an interest in reducing their pain and suffering or promoting their well-being. The agent must be able to feel guilt or shame at her own moral transgressions, and to feel anger or indignation at the transgressions of others. She must be sensitive to praise and blame, so that she can feel morally accountable for her actions.

To be responsive to ethical reasons, a moral agent needs intellectual and emotional capacities that vary with the type of ethical reasoning involved. To apply consequentialist reasoning, an agent must be able to make rough calculations of the aggregate net welfare benefits of different decisions. To apply principle-based reasoning, such as respect for rights and a regard for justice, an agent must be able to apply abstract principles to specific cases.

To apply character-based reasoning, an agent must be able to cultivate virtues, avoid vices, and be sensitive to and take responsibility for her relationships with others.

To make competent ethical decisions, a moral agent needs an understanding of ethical concepts, an understanding of cause and effect relationships, an ability to make plans, and an ability to form and carry out her intentions.

Most adult human beings have, or should have, the capacities required for moral agency. Most children have the emotional repertoire necessary for moral sensitivity but lack the reasoning and decision-making abilities needed for full moral agency. Infants and comatose human beings have none of these capacities. Some very complex animals may have rudimentary capacities for moral sensitivity, but no animals have ethical reasoning and decision-making abilities. Individual adult humans make important ethical decisions, but so do business firms, corporations, non-government organizations, municipalities, and state governments. Such organizations are not individual human beings with mental lives but are the creations of a legal system. Moral agency requires psychological capacities, such as the emotions of guilt and shame or the ability to reason ethically, and organizations have these capacities only figuratively, not literally. Yet we are inclined to praise or blame them for their decisions, and to hold them morally accountable.

5.1 Exercises

1. Formulate a definition for being a moral agent and repeat the definition aloud to help you remember it.
2. What are three important capacities of a moral agent?
3. Does a house cat have the capacities necessary to be a moral agent?
4. Should a house cat be held morally accountable for playing with (torturing) a mouse?
5. Why is there a problem with holding a business corporation (considered as a whole) morally accountable for its actions?

5.2 CAUSAL RESPONSIBILITY

The determination of causal responsibility is important in ethics for two reasons. The first reason is prediction. In advance of a decision, a moral agent needs knowledge of cause and effect to predict the probable results of her decision. The decision-maker needs to know something about what will likely happen when she chooses this course of action or that one. The second reason is retrospective. Some ethical considerations, particularly considerations of retributive and compensatory justice, require that, after the decision, we know the cause in order to assign moral accountability (praise and blame) to the correct agent.

There are several theories of what it is to be the causal condition of an outcome. The first says that the cause of an outcome is a necessary condition for the outcome. One condition is a **necessary condition** for a second if the first condition is required for the second one to happen. For example, the presence of oxygen is necessary for fire. However, a necessary condition may not be enough to produce the second condition, because the presence of further conditions may also be needed. Oxygen alone is not enough to produce fire. To say that X is necessary for Y is to say that whenever Y occurs, X must be present. In legal reasoning, this is called the "but for" test for causation. To test whether X is a necessary condition for Y, we ask: but for X (that is, without X), would Y have occurred? If the answer is yes, then X is not a necessary condition for Y. If the answer is no, then X is a necessary condition for Y. Oxygen is necessary for fire since without the presence of oxygen (but for the presence of oxygen), the fire would not have occurred.

The view that a causally responsible condition for an effect is a necessary condition for the effect has several weaknesses. One weakness is the existence of causal chains. We often see a chain of conditions all of which are necessary for the effect to happen. Members of the chain are all causal conditions of the outcome, and we have no reason to pick one of them over another. Amy's situation is like this: One, investors are unhappy. Two, the board directs the CEO. Three, the CEO instructs the cost-cutting committee. Four, Amy makes her suggestion to the committee. Five, a contact is signed. Six, the owner orders a new factory floor. Seven, the work is shoddy. Lastly, a disaster happens. All seven of these conditions are necessary for the disaster to have happened. But for any of them, there would have been no disaster.

Another problem with relying solely on a necessary condition analysis of causal responsibility is the frequent existence of other factors that would have brought about the consequence anyway. Suppose that, in our example, if Amy had not suggested outsourcing, then her colleague Ben would have done so. It would no longer be the case that, but for Amy's recommendation, the disaster would not have occurred. The committee would have followed Ben's recommendation. So, in this case, Amy's suggestion is not a necessary condition for the disaster. The outcome is overdetermined because Ben would have made the same suggestion.

A second theory of causal responsibility is the view that a cause is a sufficient condition for an effect. A **sufficient condition** is a condition that is enough to bring about the effect even if it is not required to bring about the effect. In the situation described in the last paragraph, either Amy or Ben's action would be enough, by itself, to cause the committee to consider the outsourcing strategy. Whenever the sufficient condition is present, the causal outcome is also present. We can show that X is not sufficient for Y by producing a case where the X is present, and Y is absent.

The main problem with assigning causal responsibility through sufficient conditions is that often actions are sufficient to bring about a result only given the proper combination of other background conditions. So, for example, throwing a switch is only sufficient for turning on a light bulb on the assumptions that the light bulb is not burned out, that the power is on, that the circuit connecting the switch and the bulb is not interrupted, and so on. When we count doing X as sufficient for Y, and thus that the person who did X is causally responsible for Y, it is almost always the case that doing X is sufficient for Y only given a large number of other actions by other people. And that makes it hard to sort out who is morally responsible. In our example, Amy's action is sufficient to cause the committee to consider outsourcing, but that is true only because of the background conditions: the committee has already decided to follow Amy's recommendation; the CEO has established the corporate structure to make this chain of decisions possible, and so on. The theory that causal conditions are sufficient conditions does not work in cases of joint decisions.

In contemporary society, committees, not individuals, do much of the decision-making, and committee decision-making has a way of making individual causal responsibility disappear. Suppose the cost-cutting committee in our business example has seven members and that all of those members must vote. The motion that Amy puts forward to recommend overseas production passes by five votes to two votes. Amy, of course votes in favor of the motion. The five votes in favor of the motion are jointly sufficient for the motion to pass. Amy's vote is not a necessary condition of the motion passing, because passage of the motion is over-determined; the motion would pass anyway, no matter how she voted. Had Amy voted differently, or had she later changed her vote, the motion would still have passed by four votes to three votes. Amy's vote is not a necessary element in the set of votes sufficient for passing the motion. Therefore, Amy is not causally responsible for the motion's passing. Amy's vote is not sufficient for passage of the motion because her vote would not be enough by itself to pass it. Had the vote been four to three, Amy's vote would have been causally responsible for passing the motion because her vote would have been necessary, along with three other votes, to its passage. However, Amy's vote is not a necessary condition because the motion passes five votes to two. In a case where a motion passes by two or more votes, individual causal responsibility evaporates in committee meetings.

Other situations where individual causal responsibility apparently evaporates are cases where many, many individuals contribute to bringing about bad consequence, but the individual contributions are negligible. A stock example is where one person crossing a lawn does no damage, but thousands of people crossing the lawn wears a nasty rut in it. A much more serious example is climate change, where individuals driving too much or turning their thermostats too high in winter (or too low in summer) make negligible contributions to the level of carbon dioxide in the atmosphere, yet hundreds of millions of such decisions can lead to a climate that is changed in dangerous ways. In situations like these that involve accumulative harms, assigning causal responsibility to individuals is extremely difficult or even impossible.

To further complicate these issues, we should notice that omissions can also be causal factors. A person can decide to actively do something, and this can obviously become a causal factor. Importantly, though, a person can passively decide to do nothing, and this too can become a causal factor. For example, in the Amy-example, perhaps the factory owner did not actively decide to order shoddy construction, but simply omitted to get the advice of competent engineers before adding another floor. The factory owner's omission is still a potential causal factor in the building's collapse.

5.2 Exercises

1. Formulate a definition for each of the following and repeat the definition aloud to help you remember it: (a) necessary condition, (b) sufficient condition.
2. Give an example of a condition that is not a causal factor for each of (a) a necessary condition and (b) a sufficient condition.
3. Describe a way that individual causal responsibility for the actions of an organization can disappear in a bureaucratic context.
4. Why is it very difficult to assign individual causal responsibility for accumulative harms?

5.3 MORAL ACCOUNTABILITY

We have seen how difficult it is to determine causal responsibility for an outcome. Though the notion of causation is a scientific notion, it is neither clearly defined nor easily applied. We have also seen that determining moral accountability involves a value judgment, and thus, implicitly, reasons drawn from an ethical theory. Thinking about the causal responsibility of decision-makers for outcomes is often useful in thinking about moral accountability. Nonetheless, moral accountability is an ethical notion, not a scientific one. As well as searching for an elusive determination of causal responsibility, we should also examine decision-makers and their decisions from the perspective of each of the ethical theories that we have studied. Different theories will often conflict in their assignment of moral accountability. Consequently, we must weigh these assorted considerations to arrive at one overall judgment of who is accountable. If we cannot come to an overall judgment of moral accountability, then we may still find plural judgments useful.

Identity-based reasoning holds moral agents accountable for the sort of person that they are. It recommends that we morally praise those who are virtuous in their behavior or caring and wise in their relationships. If we are virtuous in our own behavior, we are entitled to be proud of ourselves. It recommends that we morally blame those who show themselves to have vices such as envy, greed, and sloth, or who are uncaring in their relationships with others. If we are ourselves vicious or uncaring, then we should feel ashamed. Virtue ethics claims that we are morally praiseworthy if we show good character, and blameworthy if we show bad character.

Motivation-based reasoning looks first to a moral agent's self-regarding reasons for a decision. If she thinks only of her own gain and is reckless of the rights of others, then we should blame her for her behavior. If her reasoning is based on ethical principles, and if she tries her best to respect the rights of others and to fulfil her duties to them, then we should praise her for her efforts, even if she is unsuccessful. If we ourselves make decisions with the wrong motives, then we should feel guilty about what we have done.

Consequence-based moral reasoning must discover the agent who caused the outcome, and so determination of causal responsibility plays a significant role. When an agent is planning what to do, utilitarian ethical theory requires the decision-maker to predict the causal consequences of her decision. Amy, for example, should consider everyone's welfare, including offshore workers, in her decision to promote out-sourcing the company's clothing line. Consequentialist reasoning recommends that we blame or punish the agent for creating a morally bad outcome and to praise or reward him for creating a morally valuable one.

Historical theories of distributive justice, such as libertarian theories or contribution-based merit theories, need a determination of causal responsibility to decide on fair shares. Non-historical theories of distributive justice, however, do not need assessments of causal responsibility. These theories will use other, non-causal moral principles, such as Rawls's difference principle, to figure out legitimate expectations and fair shares, and are thus impervious to difficulties in assigning causal responsibility.

Governments, universities, and corporations are large organizations with complex decision-making procedures. Should we hold them morally accountable for their actions? They are all legally accountable for the consequences of their actions; for example, people can sue corporations regarding damages that they cause. If we think that moral accountability implies causal responsibility, and that causal responsibility requires that an agent's psychological state, the agent's intention, must cause the outcome, then we will be inclined to say, "No." Large organizations may have a legal personality, but not a psychological personality. Unlike people, they do not have intentions or other psychological states in a literal sense.

An individualist view about organizational moral accountability holds that only the individuals within an organization can be morally accountable, and the organization cannot be morally accountable. However, if we use a committee as a simple model of organizational decision-making, then we can see that reducing a committee decision to the decisions of individual committee members can be hugely difficult. When motions pass by more than two votes, then no one member's vote is causally responsible for the committee decision on any of the views of causal responsibility that we have discussed. Individual moral accountability appears simply to vanish in committee decision-making. We cannot reduce accountability for the committee decision to the causal responsibility of its members.

A holistic view of organizational moral accountability holds that the organization-as-a-whole, but not any of its agents and employees, is morally accountable for its decisions and for the actions of its agents and employees. The holistic view would be false if all ethical reasoning were purely motive-based. Motives are psychological states such as intentions, and as corporations do not have psychological states, it would make no sense to view corporations as ever being morally accountable. However, there are other forms of ethical reasoning, such as virtue ethics, where the existence of psychological states is less important.

From a virtue-ethics point of view, organizations can have non-mental dispositions to behave that are either virtuous or vicious. These dispositions come about because of the organization's ethical code, its compliance mechanisms, its ethical climate, its governance, and its incentive structures. From an indirect-utilitarian point of view, we can hold organizations accountable for whether their behavior promotes overall human welfare. From a rights-based point of view, we can notice that organizations enter into legal contracts with employees, suppliers, and consumers. Legal contracts are composed of promises of offer and acceptance. If we think that we are morally accountable for keeping our promises to large, complex organizations, then we should equally think that they are morally accountable for keeping their promises to us.

In applying ethical reasoning to figuring out who is morally accountable for a problematic situation and who is morally accountable for fixing the situation, we should look to a plurality of considerations drawn from different ethical approaches. Some of these considerations involve also figuring out causal responsibility, but many are solely ethical decisions.

5.3 Exercises

1. To what considerations would each of the following ethical approaches appeal in deciding whether to hold Amy morally accountable for the offshore disaster?
    a) virtue ethics
    b) a rights-based ethical approach
    c) a preference-based consequentialist approach
2. What would each of the following ethical approaches say about holding a corporation-as-a-whole morally accountable for its decisions?
    a) virtue ethics
    b) indirect utilitarianism

5.4 AUTONOMY

Suppose that her boss orders Nancy, one of the organization's IT specialists, to spy on other employees' use of social media outside of work. Nancy does not think this is right, but she does it anyway because she fears her boss will fire her. Is Nancy morally accountable for her decision to spy? The answer will depend on whether we think her decision was morally autonomous.

Moral autonomy is the capacity to govern oneself according to one's own ethical reasoning. Agents' decisions are morally autonomous when they apply to themselves (*auto* in Latin) the moral law (*nomos* in Latin). We shall start from the default position that agents' decisions are usually morally autonomous, and then ask what sorts of conditions interfere with their autonomy. In a more extreme example, suppose that one person puts a gun to a second person's head, and coerces him into making a specific decision. Here it is obvious that the second person's decision is not morally autonomous, and that we should not hold him morally accountable for his decision. Should we similarly excuse Nancy from moral accountability?

Next, consider the effects of Nancy and her boss spying on the other employees. Suddenly their activities outside of work have repercussions for the other employees. Realizing that their boss is spying on them, many employees change their private behavior and become less open with their friends on social media. Does the firm's spying wrongfully interfere with their personal lives? This brings up an ethical concept similar to, but not the same as, moral autonomy. **Personal autonomy** is the capacity to make authentic decisions about one's own life. It is the ability to choose freely one's conception of the good life, to pursue this conception, and to either endorse or change one's choices. Modern societies hold the values of personal autonomy and personal freedom in high esteem. This is a new historical development. Pre-modern communities stressed the values of following tradition and obedience to authority. Pre-modern conceptual frameworks provided few intellectual resources for community members to reflect critically on how to lead their own lives. Ethical pluralism can reveal a host of reasons both for and against the importance of the personal autonomy that our modern culture so values.

Moral autonomy is the capacity to govern oneself according one's own ethical reasoning. Any interference with people's moral autonomy is an interference with their moral agency because it interferes with their capacity to respond to ethical reasons and to make ethical decisions based on those reasons. Because "ought" implies "can," if Nancy's boss interferes with her moral autonomy in a way that prevents Nancy from making the morally correct decision, then Nancy is not morally accountable for her decision and its outcome. Interferences with moral autonomy can reduce or excuse someone's moral accountability. Some threats to moral autonomy potentially excuse agents from moral accountability. The very same sorts of conditions that can undermine moral autonomy also undermine personal autonomy.

One potential interference with autonomy is the threat of coercion. If a coercive threat is severe enough, then it overwhelms the victim's moral sensitivity, responsiveness to ethical reasons, and decision-making capacity. For example, if a gangster threatens the family of an office administrator unless she steals the petty cash for him, then we should not hold the administrator morally accountable for her decision to hand over the cash. A **coercive threat** that interferes with autonomy is a morally unjustified declaration of the intent to cause harm to the victim. A threat issued by a policeman to a crook will normally be morally justifiable and not a threat to the crook's moral autonomy. However, if a supervisor says to an employee, "Mow my lawn at home, or I will fire you at work," then this would be a morally unjustified threat that would interfere with the employee's ability to decide autonomously. Coercive threats, however, are only potential excusing conditions. We still must decide whether the threat is severe enough, compared to the importance of the decision, to say that it excuses the victim from moral accountability.

A second threat to autonomy is lying or deception. A lie is a linguistic communication which the perpetrator believes to be untrue and with which the perpetrator intends to deceive his victim. Deception is a non-linguistic action or omission that the perpetrator intentionally uses to cause her victim to believe something false. Lying and deception both interfere with their victim's capacity to make authentic, informed decisions and with their victim's ability to reason accurately. Perpetrators use both to defraud victims. Fraud is obtaining a benefit from a victim by lying or deception. Deception can undermine moral autonomy. For example, suppose a salesperson deceitfully tells a customer that some product creates no pollution, when in fact it does. Based on this false information, the customer may decide to buy the device. If the customer thinks that contributing to pollution is wrong, then the salesperson has interfered with the customer's moral autonomy.

A third threat to autonomous decision-making involves failure to disclose information. Proper reasoning requires possession of all (or else a reasonably large portion of) the information that is relevant to the decision. If a perpetrator intentionally does not disclose information to which the decision-maker is entitled, then the perpetrator compromises the victim's ability to perform sound ethical reasoning and to make good decisions. Lack of information, or possession of false information, interferes with decision-making. So, morally unjustified non-disclosure of information by others also interferes with autonomous decision-making.

A fourth threat to autonomous decision-making is a situation involving conflict of interest. Conflicts of interest occur when the self-interest of professionals, managers, agents, and board members differ from the interests of their clients, customers, principals, or organizations. Conflicts of interest occur even if members of the first group fulfil their obligations to the members of the second. For example, a financial adviser, who also sells mutual funds on commission, has a conflict of interest with her client even if the mutual fund that she recommends to her client, and for which she receives a commission, is in fact the best fund for that client. She is still in a conflict of interest situation, even when she gives the correct advice. She can mitigate this conflict of interest by disclosing her own interest in selling the fund to her client. Conflicts of interest can undermine the autonomy of decision-makers. For the client to make a truly autonomous decision, the client needs both to know the information provided by the financial adviser and to know that the financial adviser's information is reliable. To know that the financial adviser's information is reliable, the client needs to know either that it is free of conflict of interest or, at least, to know that a conflict of interest exists so that the client can critically scrutinize the advice. Conflict of interest situations like this one undermine the autonomy of the client by affecting the reliability of the information on which the client makes the decision.

A fifth threat to someone's autonomy is lack of competence in decision-making. Cognitive impairments and emotional disorders compromise people's decision-making abilities. For example, people with severe ADHD often make impulsive decisions that they later regret. We often condemn certain types of advertising to children because children's decision-making skills have not yet developed well enough for them to make autonomous choices.

A sixth threat to autonomous decision-making is someone's immersion in an oppressive conceptual framework. An **oppressive conceptual framework** is a widely shared set of strongly held and resilient beliefs about the world, values, and human nature that makes relationships of domination and subordination seem normal, natural, and unquestionable. Because unjust relationships seem so normal, natural, and unquestionable, an oppressive conceptual framework makes if difficult, if not impossible, for people to understand that certain options are unjust or otherwise immoral. Contesting an oppressive conceptual framework involves a collective, ideological, and political process such as the activities of the civil rights movement, the feminist movement, and the animal rights movement.

A seventh threat to autonomy is emotional manipulation. Just as lies, deception, non-disclosure, and conflicts of interest can affect the cognitive component of peoples' decision-making, so too can manipulation affect the emotional component. By inducing the emotion of fear, a credible, though unenforceable, coercive threat, for example, can manipulate and even overwhelm a person's decision-making. Emotional manipulators can influence other emotions such as their victims' feelings of pride, shame, guilt, solidarity, trust, or lust. Emotional manipulation, such as sexual manipulation, can influence decision-making.

Not all attempts to influence emotion, however, are threats to autonomy; many such efforts are legitimate attempts to persuade people, which, by making them emotionally aware of consequences, increase their autonomy. For example, an anti-smoking ad including a vivid and emotionally effective picture of a dreadful smoking-related disease may increase people's understanding and appreciation of the consequences of their continuing to smoke, and thus increase their ability to make an informed choice. We must make a difficult distinction between emotional manipulation and legitimate persuasion.

In considering threats to autonomy as potential excusing conditions for moral accountability, we will face making difficult distinctions. Some threats are so severe that they obviously excuse their victims from being morally accountable for their decision. Some attempts at emotional manipulation are so mild that they excuse no one. Making this distinction will always be a contestable ethical judgment.

Figure 5.1 shows a simple flow chart of the factors that go into assessing a moral person's moral accountability. After deciding that the person or organization is a moral agent, we must then ask if the agent's decision was autonomous. We do this by assessing whether there are any conditions present that interfere severely enough with the agent's decision-making to constitute excuses for making the decision. For example, we might ask if someone so misled the agent that the agent could not be reasonably expected to decide correctly what to do. Next, we should decide whether the agent is causally responsible for the outcome of her freely made decision. If so, then we should hold her accountable for making amends for her decision as a matter of compensatory or retributive justice. As we saw before, figuring out the causal responsibility of specific individuals within organizations can often be impossible because of division of labor and decision-making by committees. Nevertheless, we can still hold individuals morally accountable for their motivations and their characters. Then we continue, as in the last section, to ask about the agent's motivation and character. We should look at her motivation for her decision, and at the kind of character that she displays in making her decision. We can still blame her for the principles she is violating or the vices that she exhibits.

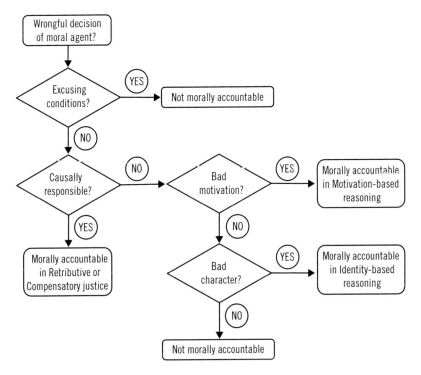

Figure 5.1: Simplified flow chart for assessing an agent's moral accountability.

5.4 Exercises

1. Formulate a definition for each of the following and repeat the definition aloud to help you remember it: (a) moral autonomy, (b) personal autonomy, (c) a coercive threat, and (d) an oppressive conceptual framework.
2. Briefly explain how each of the following can interfere with its victim's moral autonomy:
   a) a coercive threat
   b) a lie
   c) a failure of information disclosure
   d) a conflict of interest
   e) an oppressive cultural framework
   f) emotional manipulation

5.5 MORAL STANDING

In applying ethics to how we should live a life with others, we must face the question of who these others are. To whom do we owe ethical obligations? To whom are we morally accountable? Should we extend our moral concern from ourselves to other people close to us, to people in distant countries, to unborn members of future generations, to animals generally, to all living things including plants, to a concern for endangered species, or to the health of ecosystems?

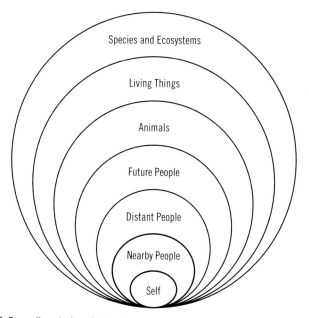

Figure 5.2: Expanding circles of ethical concern.

An entity has **moral standing** only if our ethical concern regarding the entity is for its own sake. A person might decide not to drain a small wetland on her property because she thinks that it is lovely to look at, that it makes a great bird habitat, and that it will make a great place for her children to play. Another person might decide not to drain a wetland because he thinks that a functioning ecosystem is a good thing, and that it is important to preserve its health and integrity. The second person truly regards the wetland ecosystem as having moral standing, of being morally significant for its own sake, whereas the first person does not. Both persons preserve the ecosystem, but their reasons are ethically different.

The idea of moral standing is analogous to the notion of legal standing. When a judge tries a case in a court of law, not every person or organization has the right to go into the court to make arguments about the case. The judge will allow only those persons or organizations that she regards as affected by the outcome of the trial to present arguments to the court. Such persons or organizations have legal standing in the case. Similarly, in applying ethical reasoning we consider only arguments based on the interests of those entities that we regard as having moral standing when we make ethical judgments.

Figure 5.2 represents expanding circles of ethical concern. We can think roughly, for instance, of an ethical concern for all animals as including an ethical concern for human beings, and an ethical concern for all living things as including an ethical concern for both animals and humans.

The narrowest circle of ethical concern is a circle that includes only one's self and one's own self-interest. The view that only the self has moral standing is the ethical egoism that we have looked at earlier. Most people extend their circle of ethical concern to include people who are special to them, to relatives, friends, or fellow members of a community. This concern can grow to cover fellow citizens, people who are in a sense present in both space and time, who share a common geography and who are all currently alive. More demanding is a concern for people who are not geographically present, who live in distant countries, and who are foreign and often very poor. Do people in developing countries have moral standing, and should we have the same sort of concern for their interests that we have for our fellow citizens? Questions about environmental policy are often questions about the effect of environmental degradation on people in the future, people who are not yet born. Should we extend moral standing to future generations, and if so, how? Are we ethically obliged to consider the interests of future generations in our policymaking?

Theories that assign moral standing to the self, to special people, to present people, to distant people, or to future people are anthropocentric theories. **Anthropocentric**, or human-centered, views consider only humans, members of the species *Homo sapiens*, to have moral standing. The term "anthropocentric" has the same root as the term "anthropology," which is the science of human beings. We must be careful to distinguish it from the term, "anthropomorphic," which is to attribute human behavior to a non-human entity, and from "anthropogenic," which is to attribute causation by humans to a phenomenon. Non-anthropocentric ethical views are views that extend moral standing to non-human entities: to animals, plants, or ecosystems.

Theories that are concerned with the moral standing of everything from the self through animals and plants to natural, though nonliving, objects are concerned with individual entities. These are individualistic theories of moral standing. Ecosystems, governments, universities, and corporations are not individual entities. For example, an ecosystem is a highly organized collection of both living and nonliving entities that is, in some sense, more than just the sum of its parts. Collective entities such as these require holistic theories of moral standing because they are concerned with organized wholes composed of individual entities.

The notion of an entity having moral standing relates to the important distinction between direct and indirect ethical obligations. An indirect ethical obligation is a duty regarding some other entity that an agent owes to a person. Suppose that Bob owes Alice an obligation not to burn down her forest. This is an indirect obligation regarding the forest because Bob owes the duty to Alice, not to the forest itself. If Bob owes a duty to Alice not to kick her dog, Rover, then he owes the duty to Alice and not to Rover. He has a duty to Alice not to harm her property and only an indirect duty regarding Rover, as in this diagram:

Figure 5.3: Bob has an indirect duty regarding Rover but owed to Alice.

On the other hand, a direct ethical obligation is an ethical obligation regarding some entity that an agent owes to that (perhaps non-human) entity itself. For example, Bob might have a direct obligation to the forest ecosystem not to burn it or he might have an obligation to the dog, Rover, not to kick him, as shown in this diagram:

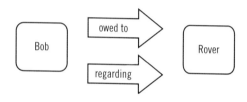

Figure 5.4: Bob has a direct duty regarding Rover and owed to Rover.

There is a conceptual connection between direct obligations, moral standing, and anthropocentric theories of ethics. For a moral agent to owe a direct obligation to a non-human entity, the non-human entity must possess moral standing. Indirect obligations do not presuppose the moral standing of the non-human world. Both types of obligation can protect the potential victim. If Bob does not kick Rover because of his duty to its owner, Alice, or if Bob does not kick Rover because he believes he has a duty to Rover, the dog, the result is the same; the dog is unharmed. However, the indirect obligation view offers less protection to the animal than does the direct obligation view. We can imagine a situation where Alice asks Bob to kick Rover. In this situation, Bob is relieved of his duty to Alice, and Bob's indirect duty to Rover no longer protects him. On the other hand, if Bob has a direct duty to Rover, then despite Alice's request, he still has a duty not to harm Rover. In general, if we assign moral standing to non-human entities, then we offer them stronger protection than if we adopt a merely anthropocentric view.

We are morally accountable only for how we treat those others who have moral standing. Rocks, for example, do not have moral standing, we do not have direct moral obligations to them, and we are not normally morally accountable for how we treat them. However, if the rocks are owned by someone, we may have an ethical obligation to the owner, and only because of that obligation are we morally accountable for how we treat the rocks.

Moral standing is theory-relative. What features are required to have moral standing will depend on which ethical theory we are applying to a situation.

Ethical egoism makes the most restrictive claim about moral standing. Only the moral agent herself has moral standing, and she need only consider her own interests. Possibly virtue ethics has the widest view of moral standing. Any aspect of the natural world from humans to ecosystems can potentially flourish and all, including the health of planet Earth, are potentially relevant to the flourishing of virtuous moral agents. A communitarian virtue ethic, however, might restrict moral standing to other members of the nearby community and perhaps to the environment in which the community is situated. To be morally considerable in the ethics of care, a creature must be the possible object of a caregiver's compassion. Infants and children are the paradigm examples, but companion animals and even specific others at great distance but with whom the caregiver has a relationship may also qualify.

The will theory of rights will grant moral standing only to those creatures that have the same capacity for moral agency, reasoning, and decision-making as competent, adult human beings. We have no correlative direct duties toward creatures who lack these capacities. So, infant humans and animals will lack moral standing in this theory. The interest theory of rights is more generous. It will grant moral standing only to creatures with significant welfare interests. Whether an organism can have such significant welfare interests will depend on its capacity to receive some important kind of psychological benefit, such as the satisfaction of a crucial desire, a capacity had by human beings and, controversially, by some complex non-human animals.

Consequentialist moral theories are quite varied in their assignment of moral standing. Experience-based utilitarianism aims to maximize pleasure and minimize pain. A creature's capacity to feel pleasure or pain depends on it having a capacity for conscious experiences, or sentience. Except for those in comas, nearly all humans are sentient. Arguably, many somewhat complex animals too are sentient, and so should receive equal consideration in any utilitarian aggregation of interests. Humans in distant parts of the globe are included, but plants, humans who do not yet exist, human organizations, and non-human ecosystems are excluded. Preference-based utilitarianism applies only to creatures that actually do have the capacity for choosing among desires. Only competent human beings and, controversially, very complex animals have this capacity. Informed preference-based utilitarianism requires that those with moral standing have the possible capacity for choosing among desires. What it maximizes is not actual preferences, but the possible preferences a creature would have if it were fully informed. We can talk of what both present-day and future generations of humans would want if fully informed.

Non-psychological consequentialist theories are eclectic in their assignments of moral standing. A teleological form of consequentialism would grant moral standing to any entity that is goal-directed, which arguably would include all moderately complex living things, such as plants and animals, and perhaps creatures such as protozoa. A holistic form of consequentialism would grant moral standing to any organized whole that can remain organized over time. Human institutions, communities, and natural ecosystems all might qualify.

We can conclude from this discussion that the question of moral standing and the question of which ethical theories apply in a situation are not separate issues. In a pluralist ethical framework, which ethical theories apply and which theories of moral standing apply must be decided together.

Ethical theory	Features required for moral standing	Possible examples
Ethical egoism	Having a self and being self-interested	Competent *Homo sapiens*
Virtue ethics	Having the ability to flourish	Humans, animals, nations, communities, ecosystems
Communitarian virtue ethics	Being a member of the community	Nearby people and their environment
Care ethics	Being a possible object of compassion and loving care	Infants, children, household pets, family, friends
Will theory of rights	Capacity for agency, reasoning, decision-making	Competent *Homo sapiens*
Interest theory of rights	Capacity for receiving a psychological benefit	Quite complex animals including humans
Contractarian ethical egoism	Ability to make and keep contracts	Competent *Homo sapiens*
Experience-based utilitarianism	Capacity for conscious experiences	Somewhat complex animals, nearly all humans
Preference-based utilitarianism	Actual capacity for choosing among desires	Competent *Homo sapiens*, very complex animals
Informed preference-based utilitarianism	Possible capacity for choosing among desires	Present and future generations of *Homo sapiens*
Teleological consequentialism	Being goal-directed	Living things
Holistic consequentialism	Remaining an organized whole through time	Human institutions, ecosystems

Table 5.1: A rough summary and outline of the features required for moral standing by twelve different ethical theories, with examples.

5.5 Exercises

1. Formulate a definition for each of the following and repeat the definition aloud to help you remember it: (a) moral standing, and (b) an anthropocentric view of moral standing.
2. Give an example, different from the ones in the text, that illustrates the difference between a direct and an indirect ethical obligation.
3. Set aside your own ethical views on animals and business corporations, and consider which of the ethical approaches in the left column of Table 5.1 would assign moral standing to (a) a laying hen, (b) an adult chimpanzee, and (c) the Apple computer company.
4. Set aside your own views on the problem of abortion and the moral status of the fetus, and consider which of the ethical approaches in the left column of Table 5.1 would assign moral standing to (a) a human fetus at conception, (b) a human fetus when it becomes viable, and (c) a human infant at birth.

CHAPTER 6

RESOLVING CONFLICT BETWEEN MORAL REASONS

THERE ARE THREE WAYS TO APPROACH THE QUESTION OF HOW BEST to live in a world full of both human and non-human others. Each of us should strive to become a good person, should act based on ethical principles, and should struggle to create what is morally valuable. The three approaches give distinct types of reasons to act. Sometimes these reasons align and point to the same decision. But often they conflict in their recommendations. Then what should we do?

People make judgments about what to do all the time, and they make these judgments for reasons. Here it is important that the word "reasons" be in the plural. In almost any decision any of us have ever made, we can find reasons for and against an action. Some reasons are stronger than others, and sometimes one reason may have overriding importance. Nevertheless, people usually judge what is best and decide what to do, not for one reason, but according to the balance of several reasons.

Figure 6.1: Usually, more that one reason contributes to our judgment of what is best and to our decision about how to act.

This chapter is about resolving moral conflicts by combining moral reasons. Problems arise because ethical theory is irreducibly plural. The three main approaches to ethics give rise to a large variety of ethical theories. Each theory points to different features of a situation that may be relevant to deciding what to do. It is best not to regard ethical theories as universal moral laws. Understood as strict universal laws, moral theories often contradict one another, rather than balance against one another. For instance, suppose there were a strict moral law to always keep promises and a strict moral law to always aid the suffering. For someone faced with helping a stricken senior citizen while hurrying to keep a promised lunch date, these strict moral laws would contradict one another. We can see the way different types of ethical considerations balance with one another in some thought-experiments proposed by philosophers. These cases are abstract and unrealistic, but they nicely illustrate how considerations involving consequences, intentions, and character can come into conflict.

The notion of balancing ethical reasons, as though ethical reasons had weights and were put on a balance scale, is a metaphor, and it is best not to take it too seriously. There are structural problems with the notion of weighing moral reasons. We can avoid these problems if we understand moral reasoning as uncertain and probabilistic. This chapter closes by recommending that it is better to think of ethical theories as giving fallible advice about what it is best to do.

6.1 ETHICAL PLURALISM

Some types of ethical considerations pertain to the identity and character of the decision-maker. Some pertain to the motivation of the decision-maker and the principles that she follows. Others pertain to judging the consequences of implementing the decision. All these types of ethical considerations can provide reasons for or against a specific decision. Additionally, these general approaches to an ethical decision further subdivide into different ethical theories, as shown again in Figure 6.2.

Ethical theories are ways of systematizing ethical reasons that philosophers have developed over the many centuries during which philosophers have been thinking about ethical problems. Philosophers have formulated each type of ethical theory in response to weaknesses that they discovered in other theories. Applied ethics should avoid focusing on just one theory and instead use all these theories to obtain a complete picture of the ethical issues facing a decision-maker. The discoveries made during academic debates help to assess the strengths and weaknesses of the different theories and to weigh the ethical reasons for and against specific decisions.

Ethical pluralism is the view that each of us should make ethical decisions by considering and balancing the (often-conflicting) ethical reasons that follow from more than one ethical theory, and then judging how to proceed. It contrasts with ethical monism, which is the view that moral agents should make all their ethical decisions by applying just one specific theory such as, for example, utilitarianism. Ethical pluralism gives us a picture of ethical decision-making in which different ethical theories give the decision-maker ethical reasons of varying strengths that point for and against the overall advice, "Yes, do it," or "No, don't do it." By reflecting critically on the strengths and weaknesses of these reasons, weighing them, and balancing them, the decision-maker can decide what to do. Unfortunately, philosophy does not supply a recipe for how exactly to balance the various ethical reasons affecting the decision. Making a final judgment is a high-level skill analogous to the skill shown by a judge balancing the evidence and arguments presented in a courtroom trial.

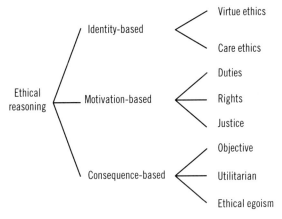

Figure 6.2: A taxonomy of ethical reasoning showing some of the different ethical theories that philosophers have developed to systematize ethical reasoning.

A useful analogy is to the way the board of directors of a large business decides about, for example, launching a new product. The Chief Ethics Officer calls a meeting of representatives from all ethical theories and listens to their advice, just as a regular Chief Executive Officer listens to the advice of her vice-presidents of sales, finance, production, etc. All the representatives look at the situation from the point of view of their ethical theory and then give reasons for and against potential decisions. The CEO weighs the reasons advanced from each point of view and makes a judgment about the best action to take. Again, the CEO has no fixed decision procedure to follow, no algorithm that will give the best answer in every case. Instead, the CEO must use experience and judgment to decide. The decision will be a better one because of the input from all the various ethical approaches.

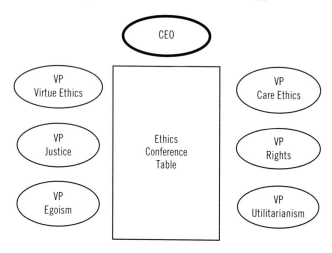

Figure 6.3: The Chief Ethics Officer (CEO) decides after hearing from all divisions of ethical theory.

Notice that this picture of ethical decision-making is ethical pluralist, not ethical relativist. Ethical pluralism does not say that the decision is the right one relative to one ethical theory, the wrong one relative to another, and that the disagreement has no rational resolution. It does not say, for example, that a decision may be right according to utilitarianism and wrong according to virtue ethics, and that we can never resolve the issue. Instead, ethical pluralism says that, though there is no explicit decision procedure or algorithm for making a final judgment, moral agents can nonetheless make such a judgment, and it will be a better one for having considered the situation from all ethical points of view. The various ethical considerations sometimes conflict with one another. Nevertheless, the resulting overall ethical decision is a better one than the alternatives. The claim that it is a better decision is universally true, not just true relative to some specific ethical theory.

Sometimes the recommendations of different theories coincide, and there is no problem. However, sometimes recommendations conflict. On the face of it, if two different ethical theories entail different conclusions about how to act, then either they contradict one another, and the conversation between points of view that is envisioned by ethical pluralism comes to a jarring halt, or one recommendation is just wrong.

Recall the case of the Truth-teller and the Axe-murderer from the chapter on principles and rights. Truth-teller's roommate is in her room. A would-be murderer comes to the door and asks the Truth-teller if his roommate is at home. Truth-teller believes that he has a duty to always tell the truth to others, no matter what the consequences. Truth-teller believes that, correspondingly, the murderer has a right to hear the truth from him. Truth-teller tells the murderer that his roommate is in, believing that, since he, the Truth-teller, had good intentions, then he, the Truth-teller, should not be morally condemned for the ensuing bloodshed. Truth-teller owes this duty to tell the truth to the murderer, and this duty creates a correlative right of the murderer to hear the truth. However, the consequences of truth-telling are so awful, and the consequences of lying so much better, that the principle of respecting the right to be told the truth is overridden in this context.

In the context of lying to an Axe-murderer, the duty not to lie is outweighed by utilitarian intuitions. Yet, any sort of utilitarian duty to maximize happiness will also have contexts where it fails to hold. Maximizing aggregate preference satisfaction will sometimes violate moral rights. Recall the Transplant Case (Thomson 1976), where a surgeon decides to maximize the moral value of continued life by removing the organs from an unsuspecting person and transplanting them into five needy people, saving five lives but losing one. This conclusion violates strongly held intuitions about what is morally permissible and shows that the utilitarian moral law cannot be universal and exceptionless.

Rather than saying that the duty not to lie and the obligation not to permit harm contradict one another, it is better to interpret the duty not to lie as a moral reason or an ethical consideration that carries a certain metaphorical weight. The recommendation not to lie can be outweighed by other recommendations. In this case, consequentialist considerations such as the bloody death of Truth-teller's roommate, and the virtue ethics consideration that truth-telling requires Truth-teller to have an overly rigid character and to show little wisdom, together outweigh Kant's reason to tell the truth. Rather than interpreting utilitarianism as putting forward the universal moral law that agents should always maximize utility, it is better to think of maximizing utility as a recommendation that is mostly good advice, but which can be outweighed by other considerations. The surgeon maximizes aggregate utility by satisfying the preferences of five people, but the rights of the unsuspecting victim outweigh this utilitarian consideration.

In the Truth-teller and the Axe-murderer case, maximizing utility outweighs the right of the Axe-murderer to hear the truth.

When applying ethical theories to making decisions, we should treat ethical theories, not as rules that tell us what we must do, but as recommendations that offer us advice about what to do. Ethical rules do not give us rules that can sometimes contradict one another, but instead give us recommendations that sometimes must be balanced against one another.

6.1 Exercises

1. Formulate a definition for each of the following and repeat the definition aloud to help you remember it: (a) ethical theory and (b) ethical pluralism.
2. Describe an example of moral reasoning that takes into account several different types of ethical consideration.
3. Briefly explain why ethical pluralism is not the same as ethical relativism.
4. Why is it difficult to formulate a strict universal moral law that holds without exception?
5. Construct another case where rigid respect for rights is overridden by strongly held consequentialist intuitions.
6. Construct another case where maximizing utility is trumped by respecting moral rights.
7. Construct a case where maximizing the average level of welfare would violate stronger concerns of social justice.
8. Analyze what Jim should do in this philosophically famous case invented by the English philosopher Bernard Williams (Smart & Williams 1973, 98–99). A death squad captures Jim while he is on a botanical expedition in a South American country. His captors take him to a village where the death squad have twenty villagers lined up against a wall with their hands tied. The leader of the squad makes Jim the following proposition: "If you shoot this one, I will let the others go free. If you do not, then I will kill them all."

6.2 COMBINING MORAL REASONS

The three major approaches to leading a good life are independent of one another and sometimes give conflicting recommendations. If we think of them as grounding universal moral laws, then they will generate contradictions.

Contradictions end debate. Since there is no rational way to decide on one law rather than the other, then all that remains is for their proponents to fight it out. A better way to think of conflicting ethical considerations is to think of them as having different degrees of normative force pointing in different directions. The strengths of different moral reasons can be combined and balanced against one another to achieve a reasonable resolution. This way of looking at conflicts still permits rational debate about the relative strengths of the relevant reasons, rather than immediately leading to irrational warfare.

Philosophers have invented and studied many situations in which moral reasons of different types must be weighed against one another. These situations illustrate the sorts of problems that arise when reasoning in an ethically pluralist framework. Some of these cases are described below. In most of the situations there is a choice between two outcomes. Within a broadly utilitarian approach, there is no moral difference between the two outcomes; however, when utilitarian reasons are combined with other non-utilitarian reasons, a difference appears.

The interactions between different ethical approaches are revealed by variants of the philosophically famous Trolley Problem. While trolley problems are abstract and unrealistic, they do clearly illustrate conflicting moral considerations. Sometimes an agent acts in such a way as to produce unintended consequences. Suppose the Switch-person at a Y-junction in the tracks sees a runaway trolley approaching. The trolley will run over an innocent person that she can see on the tracks ahead. To save that person, she diverts the trolley onto another track, as in Figure 6.4.

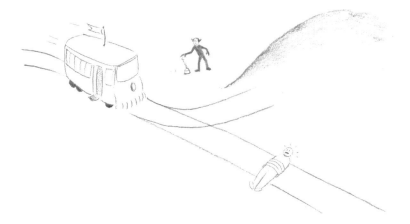

Figure 6.4: Switch-person, who is unable to see what lies on the detour, diverts the trolley and saves the innocent victim.

Because of the terrain, what she cannot see is that there are five people on the other track. She cannot foresee that they will all die as an unintended consequence of her act, as in Figure 6.5. From a consequentialist point of view, her action to divert the trolley is a bad one because she causes five deaths instead of allowing one. But her intentions were good. She intended to respect the rights of the one person that she knew of, but she unintentionally caused the deaths of five persons. She did not cause these five deaths because she was motivated by bad principles. The principle that she acted on was a sound moral principle. Mostly in situations like this, our overall judgment will be to excuse the Switch-person because considerations regarding her good intentions outweigh considerations regarding the increased harm done.

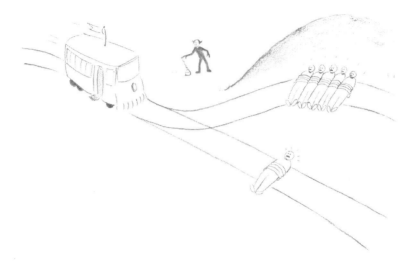

Figure 6.5: The unintended consequence of Switch-person's act is the death of five other concealed victims.

In the last example, it was impossible for her to foresee the death of the five. Suppose, instead, that with very little time and effort, she could have looked round the hill and seen that there are five people on the other track. If she did not look, then she would be negligent. Such negligence is a sign of bad character, a vice. Our overall moral judgment might change and now be against excusing her.

Suppose now that there is a person on the detour that the Switch-person wants dead. She diverts the runaway trolley onto the detour, killing this person, as in Figure 6.6. This is wrong.

RESOLVING CONFLICT BETWEEN MORAL REASONS | 127

Figure 6.6: Switch-person intentionally diverts the runaway trolley onto the detour and onto her victim. This is an act and a killing.

Compare this to a slightly different case in which the person whom the Switch-person wants dead is in the path of the trolley, as in Figure 6.7. She could easily throw the switch, divert the trolley to the detour, and save the other person. She does not, and her failure to act causes the person to die. This is also wrong.

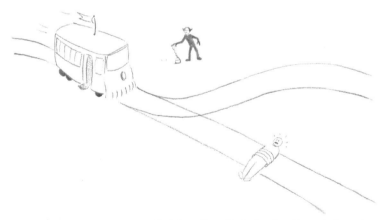

Figure 6.7: Switch-person intentionally fails to divert the trolley from the main line, allowing the trolley to run over her victim. This is an omission and a letting-die.

There is, however, a difference. In the first case the Switch-person performs an act that causes the death. This act is a killing. In the second case, the Switch-person's failure to act causes the death. This omission is a letting-die. Omitting to switch the track is just as much a cause of the death as is the act of switching in the killing case. But for the Switch-person's failure to switch the track, the victim would not have died. The omission is enough to bring about the victim's death. The omission is both necessary and sufficient to cause the victim's death. Both the killing and the letting-die cause the victim's death.

On a consequentialist view, there is no difference between killing and letting die since their causal consequences are the same. On a rights-based view, however, there is a difference. A killing is a violation of a negative right, the negative right not to have one's life interfered with. A letting-die is not a violation of a negative right. Instead it is a violation of a positive right, the positive right to assistance from others. Mostly, rights not to be interfered with are stronger than rights to assistance. Moreover, the sort of person who would aggressively kill another seems more vicious than the sort of person who would passively allow another person to be killed without rescuing them. Both killings and lettings-die are wrong, but killings are usually worse.

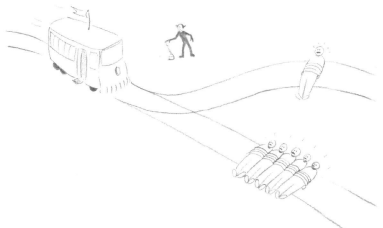

Figure 6.8: The best-known version of the Trolley Case: A runaway trolley will kill five unless Switch-person diverts it onto one.

In the original, and most famous, Trolley Case (Thomson 1976), the Switch-person must decide whether to allow the runaway trolley to proceed along the main line and run over five innocents or to divert the trolley onto the detour where it will run over one innocent person, as in Figure 6.8. According to the consequentialist approach, the right action is obvious; save five at the expense of one. According to the rights-based approach, this action respects the positive rights of the five to assistance but violates the negative right of the one to not have his life taken. On the other hand, the Switch-person's intention is not to kill the one; her intention is to save the five, but with the unintended, though easily foreseeable, consequence of killing the one. Her intention is not to violate anyone's rights and she is not acting on the false principle that it is permissible to violate someone's right to life. Yet diverting the trolley will still be a killing on the part of the Switch-person.

The Trolley Case appears to be a moral dilemma, where all outcomes are bad, rather than a moral problem with a best solution. A way out of the dilemma may be the Doctrine of the Double Effect, which is suggested in Roman Catholic jurisprudence. The suggestion is that an otherwise evil act is morally permissible if it meets four criteria: (1) one of the possible outcomes must be a good effect, (2) the agent foresees but does not directly intend the evil effect, (3) the good effect is produced directly by the action, and not by means of the bad effect, and (4) the good consequence outweighs the evil consequence. Switching the track satisfies the Doctrine of the Double Effect because (1) saving five is good, (2) the Switch-person does not intend to kill the one, (3) she does it directly by switching the track and not by means of killing the one, and (4) five saved outweighs one saved. The Doctrine of the Double Effect indicates the many ethical considerations that must be weighed against one another in the Trolley Case.

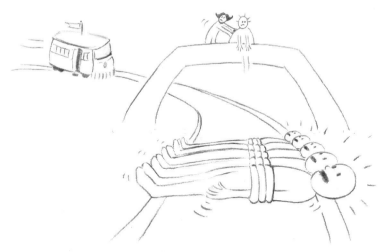

Figure 6.9: Switch-person can save five by pushing the large man in front of the runaway trolley.

Another variant, the Footbridge Case, appears to contrast interestingly with the original Trolley Case. In this case, shown in Figure 6.9, the Switch-person is on a footbridge over the track. The runaway trolley is heading toward five innocents who cannot get out of the way. There is no side-track and no lever to switch. Instead, there is a large man on the footbridge with her. She knows a lot about trolleys, and she knows that if she jumps in front of the trolley, then she will not be heavy enough to stop it from hitting the five. However, she does know that the large man is heavy enough to stop the trolley and, if he landed on the tracks, then his dead body would save the five. Should she push him over the side of the footbridge and into the path of the trolley, thereby saving five and killing one?

According to the consequentialist approach, there is no difference between the two cases. However, experimental philosophers have found that, if put in the position of the Switch-person, more people are willing to throw the lever to save five and kill one than are willing to push the large man off the footbridge to save five and kill one. By studying brain-scans of people presented with the two cases, they have discovered that the Trolley Case provokes more activity in deliberative reasoning parts of the brain than does the Footbridge Case, whereas the Footbridge Case provokes more activity in emotional parts of the brain than does the Trolley Case (Greene 2014, 121–24). Deliberative reasoning attends to saving five at the expense of one; emotion attends to the idea of directly touching and pushing an innocent person off the bridge as a means of saving five. The deliberation is consequentialist, whereas the emotional response is to the direct violation of the large man's negative rights and the intention to use him as a means rather than an end-in-himself.

Though saving five by switching the track may satisfy the Double Effect criterion, saving the five by pushing the one may not. Though pushing the one (1) has a good effect that (2) is perhaps not directly intended, and (4) the good effects outweigh the bad, it remains that the good effect is only achieved by means of the bad effect. So, condition (3) is not satisfied in the Footbridge Case, and this is a moral difference between it and the original Trolley Case.

Trolley cases are abstract and unrealistic and (hopefully) unlikely to occur. But they do illustrate the ways in which ethical considerations can come into conflict with one another when we apply ethical reasoning in our lives.

6.2 Exercises

1. Give examples of (a) unintended and unforeseen consequences, (b) unintended and foreseeable consequences, (c) an omission with causal consequences, and (d) using a person as a means rather than an end-in-herself.

2. Analyze the moral difference between active euthanasia (e.g., administering a life-ending injection) and passive euthanasia (e.g., withdrawing life support).
3. Analyze the moral difference between performing an abortion to save a pregnant mother's life and performing a hysterectomy (surgical removal of the womb) on a pregnant woman with a life-threatening cancer.
4. Consider another trolley case, the Trapdoor Case, in which a large man is standing on a trapdoor on the footbridge and Switch-person controls a lever that will open the trapdoor. Pulling the lever will drop the large man in front of the runaway trolley, killing him, but saving five innocents. Is there a moral difference between this case and the previous Footbridge Case, and, if so, what is it? (NB: This is a very difficult case.)
5. Go to the website < https://www.philosophyexperiments.com/> and try some of the activities, especially (a) "Should you kill the fat man?," (b) "Should you kill the backpacker?," (c) "Peter Singer and the Drowning Child," (d) "Would you eat your cat?," and (e) "Morality Play."

6.3 BALANCING MORAL REASONS

Applying independent ethical considerations to ethical decisions frequently produces conflicting judgments. One philosopher to explicitly acknowledge this problem was W.D. Ross (see Chapter 3). In his theory of *prima facie* duties, beneficence, fidelity, gratitude, justice, non-maleficence, reparation, and self-improvement can conflict with one another. If someone makes a promise to meet a friend for lunch, then he has a *prima facie* duty of fidelity to keep his promise. If, on the way to meet his friend, he sees a senior citizen who needs help getting to the hospital, then he has a *prima facie* duty of beneficence to help the person in trouble. The two *prima facie* duties conflict; he cannot both keep his promise to his friend and be helpful to the person needing medical attention. Yet he needs to know what his overall duty is.

Conceiving of *prima facie* duties as conflicting exception-free moral rules produces contradictions. From the fidelity premise that a moral agent must always keep his promises, it follows logically that he should meet his friend for lunch. From the beneficence premise that an agent should always produce the best consequences, it follows that he should help the senior to the hospital. The second premise does not invalidate the previous deduction; instead, it produces a contradiction, and a contradiction cannot tell him his overall duty.

Ross was aware of this problem and claimed that moral agents must use an intuitive process of balancing to resolve conflicts between *prima facie* duties. Each *prima facie* duty contributes to determining the agent's overall duty but does not determine it. He said that the process of determining an overall duty from the various contributory, *prima facie*, duties was a process of intuitive balancing that did not produce infallible answers (Ross and Stratton-Lake 2002, 42).

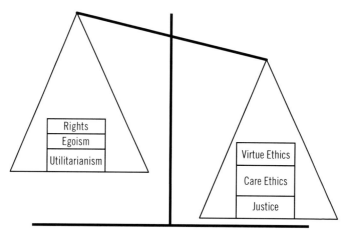

Figure 6.10: The metaphorical weighing of reasons. A decision-maker balances several ethical considerations for and against. The considerations are drawn from a plurality of ethical theories and have different weights.

This claim suggests the common view that moral reasons combine as though they were being weighed against one another on a balance scale. The metaphor of weighing is attractive because it agrees with the intuition that, when moral reasons conflict, then they do not logically contradict one another. Rather, the weight of one reason subtracts from the weight of the other and decreases our certainty that the conclusion is the right one. So, for example, in the promise-keeping case, the moral agent would probably conclude that the overall balance of reasons favored helping the senior to the hospital. The weight of the promise does not go away; it is merely outweighed by the weight of his *prima facie* duty of beneficence.

It is important to remember that this weighing model is a metaphor. Moral agents do not literally have a small set of balance scales inside their brains, and moral reasons do not literally have weights in the way that stones, teacups, and elephants have weights. It is true that ethical decision-makers can do mental addition and subtraction of the ethical pros and cons of an action, just as decision-makers can do logical deductions and find contradictions. However, the weighing metaphor breaks down in two crucial ways.

First, the weights of reasons have an upper bound, while the weights of physical objects do not. Suppose that Iris is in a situation where she must press either the dark button, which will save the life of Ms. White, or the light button, which does nothing. Saving Ms. White is an extremely strong reason to press the dark button. It makes Iris almost certain that, given her options, she ought to press the dark button. She has a decisive reason to press the dark button. Let us say that Iris is 99% certain that she should press the dark button.

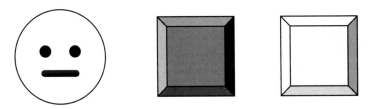

Figure 6.11: By pressing the dark button, Iris can save Ms. White. She is 99% confident that pressing the dark button is what she should do.

Now suppose that Iris comes to realize that, by pressing the dark button, she can save the lives of two persons, Ms. White and Mr. Grey, but by pressing the light button, she will save no one. Iris now has two reasons for pressing the dark button. Already Iris was nearly certain what she ought to do, and now she is a little bit more so. If saving Ms. White's life makes Iris 99% confident that she ought to push the dark button, and she learns that pushing the dark button will also save Mr. Grey's life, she does not become twice as confident that she should push the dark button. Her confidence that she should press the dark button will change very little. Perhaps now Iris is 99.9% certain that she should press the dark button. Iris is clearly not 198% certain that she should press the dark button. Just saving Ms. White is already a decisive reason for pressing the dark button. There is an upper bound to how confident she can become. Iris's degree of confidence that she should press the dark button, given that it will save Ms. White and that it will save Mr. Grey, is not equal to the sum of her degree of confidence that she should press the dark button given that doing so will save Ms. White plus her degree of confidence that she should press the dark button given that it will save Mr. Grey.

Saving the second person offers only a little additional weight to her reasons for pressing the dark button. Yet, if it had not been the case that Iris was already very confident that she ought to press the dark button to save Ms. White, then saving Mr. Grey would have added a great deal of weight to her reasons for pressing the dark button. In the sequential picture just described, it may seem natural to say that the contribution of saving Ms. White was 99% and the incremental contribution of saving Mr. Grey was just 0.9%. However, this picture of first Ms. White and second Mr. Grey is highly arbitrary and fails to give their interests equal consideration. The information about Mr. Grey is ethically identical to the information about Ms. White. Suppose Iris had considered Mr. Grey first and Ms. White second. Then the incremental contribution of their interests would be reversed. In the absence of a historical timeline, the order in which Iris considers their interests is morally arbitrary, and in its presence, the order is contingent in a morally irrelevant way.

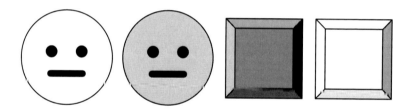

Figure 6.12: By pressing the dark button, Iris can save both Ms. White and Mr. Grey. She is 99.9% certain, not 198% certain, that she should press the dark button.

Second, reasons are context-dependent while weights are not. Reasons are always reasons for a conclusion. A fundamental function of moral reasoning is to help us come to conclusions about what we ought to do. Thus, the normative force of a moral reason is always relative to the conclusion that it supports. A contributory moral reason does not have an unconditional strength that remains constant no matter what conclusion we apply it toward. For example, suppose that Iris is in a situation where she must press either the dark button, which will save the life of Ms. White, or the light button, which does nothing. That Iris should save Ms. White gives a great deal of support to the conclusion that Iris ought to press the dark button, but it gives no support at all to the conclusion that she ought to give money to buy mosquito nets through the Against Malaria Foundation, or to perform any other worthy action. A reason, such as saving the life of Ms. White, does not have a fixed weight that it carries with it from one context, such as pressing the dark button, to another context, such as donating to AMF. Iris cannot detach a contributory reason for a conclusion from one context, transfer it to another, and expect its normative force to remain constant (Dancy 2004). Instead, if there is any way to measure something like the weight of a *prima facie* or contributory moral reason, then it will apply to pairs of reasons and conclusions. It will measure the support given to a conclusion by a reason.

There are major structural differences between measuring the weights of physical objects and measuring the support given by reasons to conclusions. In applying ethics to complicated situations, the weighing metaphor can be a misleading guide to combining moral reasons.

6.3 Exercises

1. Why is the weighing model of moral reasons more plausible, on the face of it, than the logical deduction model?
2. Why is there an upper bound to any measure of the support that a reason can offer to a conclusion?
3. What is the difference between the weight of a physical object in different contexts and the weight of a reason in the context of different conclusions?

6.4 FALLIBLE MORAL REASONING

The idea that ethical obligations are *prima facie* rather than absolute and universal implicitly suggested the analogy between the weights of reasons and the weights of physical objects. However, W.D. Ross also explicitly suggested an analogy between moral reasoning and probabilistic reasoning and observed that reflection on *prima facie* duties will merely increase the likelihood of doing the right thing. When we reflect on the good qualities of a poem, we do not reach an overall judgment on its merit by logical reasoning from its features. Rather, he writes, "Both in this and in the moral case we have *more or less probable* opinions which are not logically justified conclusions from the general principles that are recognized as self-evident" (Ross and Stratton-Lake 2002, 31; emphasis added). He also noted an analogy between reasoning about moral obligations and reasoning about self-interest. He said that we never know

> ... what act will in the long run be to our advantage. Yet it is certain that we are *more likely in general* to secure our advantage if

we estimate to the best of our ability *the probable tendencies* of our actions in this respect, than if we act on caprice. And similarly we *are more likely to do our duty* if we reflect to the best of our ability on the *prima facie* rightness or wrongness of various possible acts in virtue of the characteristics we perceive them to have, than if we act without reflection. With *this greater likelihood* we must be content. (Ross and Stratton-Lake 2002, 31–32; emphasis added)

The implication of these suggestions is that a *prima facie* duty of fidelity, for example, may not be universal and exception-free, such as the assertion that "In all situations, it is right to keep promises," but instead may be probabilistic, such as the advice that "In most situations, it is right to keep promises."

Ross's suggestion would avoid turning moral conflicts into moral contradictions. In the promise-keeping versus helping-out example, a probabilistic version of the duty of fidelity does not contradict a probabilistic version of the duty of beneficence that says, "Most likely, if someone needs help from one of us, then we should do so." Moral reasoning, like scientific reasoning about statistical evidence and legal reasoning about fault in tort law, involves balancing probabilities, not deductive argument.

Probabilistic moral generalities are not exceptionless moral rules. Instead they are recommendations or advice about what moral agents should probably do in order to do what they ought to do. They could be understood as advice from philosophers such as Confucius, Aristotle, Kant, and Bentham. They express recommendations, based on the various ethical approaches, about the way agents probably ought to act. Instead of taking Kant to be asserting that a person should never lie, we should reinterpret him to be expressing the advice that it is highly likely that a person should not lie.

Probabilistic moral generalities play an advisory role in moral reasoning. They are pedagogical tools in the learning of moral competence, they are useful tools in moral deliberation, they can clarify moral disagreements, and they are heuristic tools for recognizing the ethically salient features of problematic situations. They are not simple statistical generalizations about moral activity. They find justifications in human reason, human emotional responses, consistency with considered moral judgments, and the testimony of wise people.

Probability is used to measure uncertainty in all sorts of ways. If a fair coin is thrown, it is equally likely that each of the two sides will land up. Which side will land up is uncertain, but, if it is a fair coin, then the probability that the coin will show heads is 1/2. If a scientist were to do an experiment involving many coin tosses, then the relative frequency of heads would be approximately 1/2. The scientist's degree of confidence that the next coin will be a head ought to match the relative frequency of heads that resulted from her experiment. This is not a logical entailment but is a requirement of rationality. A scientist can also make a one-off prediction and say how confident she is that her prediction is correct. For example, an economist could say that she is 90% certain that there will be a recession next year. She is not generalizing from many samples of recessions. Instead, she is examining various economic indicators to produce a prediction about a unique event, and then using a probability measure to say how confident she is that the unique event will occur. By analogy to this sort of scientific reasoning, moral reasoning is reasoning about the appropriate degree of confidence to have in the rightness or wrongness of a decision.

Probabilities have the right sort of structure to measure the support given to a moral conclusion by a moral reason. Recall that the magnitude of the support that a moral reason gives to a conclusion about the morally right decision to make approaches an upper bound as the support offered by the reason becomes more decisive. Probabilities have this same structural feature. Probabilities have an upper bound of one, which implies absolute certainty. Very few things are totally certain, except perhaps the truths of logic and mathematics. However, our confidence in our judgments tends to approach the value of one the more certain we are in the judgment. Similarly, probabilities, considered as a measure of rational support, do have an upper bound. Only a judgment that is completely certain has a probability of one.

Probabilities also have the second feature of context dependence, provided they are understood to be conditional probabilities. The **conditional probability** of a judgment being true is the probability of the judgment being true on the assumption that some other judgment is true. Conditional probabilities are different from the more familiar unconditional probabilities. For example, suppose someone rolls a fair die behind a screen and asks another person, who cannot see the die, what is the probability of the die showing a five. The second person will say the probability is 1/6. This is her theoretical prediction based on knowing that each of the six possible numbers is equiprobable. If asked how confident that she is that the face showing is a five, she will say that she is 16.66% (1/6) confident that it is a five. Her degree of confidence in the outcome will determine her betting behavior. If her degree of confidence did not track her predictions about outcomes, then she would probably lose money playing games of chance. 0.1666 or 1/6 is the *unconditional* probability that the die shows a five.

Now suppose that the die roller truthfully tells her that the die is showing an odd number, and again asks her what is the probability that the die shows a five. She now recalculates and makes another prediction. If the die is showing an odd number, then it must be showing a one, a three, or a five. As far as she knows, it has an equal chance of showing any one of these three numbers, so the probability that it is showing a five is 1/3. Given the information that the fair die is showing an odd number, the probability that it is showing a five is 1/3. The probability that it is showing a five, on the assumption that it is showing an odd number, is 1/3. 1/3 is the *conditional* probability that the die is showing a five, given that it is showing an odd number. This predicted conditional probability tells her the degree of confidence, 33.33% in percentage terms, that she should have in the die showing a five on the assumption that the die is showing an odd number. It is this degree of confidence that should now govern her betting behavior.

Now suppose that the die-roller, having told her that the die is showing an odd number, asks her what is the probability that the die is showing a four. Four is not an odd number, so she will reply that the probability is zero. The same assumption, that the die shows an odd number, should give her a 33.33% degree of confidence that the die is showing a five, and a zero degree of confidence that the die is showing a four. The same piece of information, that the die is showing an odd number, offers different levels of support to different conclusions. This is analogous to the context relativity of moral reasons.

The measure of the support that a reason gives to a conclusion is a measure of the confidence that Iris should have in concluding that she should do an act, which is pressing the dark button, on the assumption that the reason, which is that doing so will save Ms. White, is true. This is a measure of Iris's confidence that she should press the dark button *given* that doing so would save Ms. White, or on the *condition* that doing so would save Ms. White. The best measure for this is a conditional probability, which is defined over two propositions, the reason and the conclusion. We can measure this degree of support by using the conditional probabilities of the beliefs that are our conclusions given the beliefs that are our contributory reasons.

The picture of ethical reasoning that emerges is one of drawing uncertain conclusions using fallible moral reasoning based on fallible moral advice or on fallible morally relevant information. Yet it has the advantage of being a truer picture of our moral life than is the picture of morality governed by universal, exceptionless moral rules. For a moral agent to act for moral reasons, she should be confident that the reasons for her decision are good ones. At this point, none of us should have any confidence that any universal moral law is true. The idea that, for example, all persons, in all contexts, and on all occasions should keep promises has no credibility at all. There are just too many exceptions. A rational moral agent should have zero confidence in any absolute universal moral principle, so no absolute moral principle can guide her actions. However, a rational moral agent's confidence in a fallible piece of advice, such as "The conditional probability that such-and-such is the right thing to do given that it maximizes happiness is high," should itself be quite high. As a piece of wise advice, it is a platitude. So, people can have confidence in fallible moral generalities, and fallible moral generalities can motivate people to act. Probability can be a guide to life.

Terms such as "nearly always" and "almost always" capture the moral force of fidelity and beneficence, and of the advice of Kant and Bentham, without making ethics into a kind of enterprise that has no serious implications for how people should behave. In the earlier example of the person breaking a promise to meet for lunch in order to aid a stricken senior citizen, the person's moral reasoning should go like this:

1. Nearly always, I ought to keep my promise to meet for lunch, given that I have promised to do so. (high conditional probability)
2. Almost always, I ought to stop and help, given that a senior citizen needs assistance. (even higher conditional probability)
3. Therefore, more probably than not I ought to stop and help, given both my promise and the senior's situation.
4. Therefore, given the overall situation, more probably than not, I ought to stop and help.

This conclusion has strong implications for how the person should act. Given that more probably than not she ought to stop and help, it would be irrational for her to conclude that she ought to do something else instead.

The conclusion that moral reasoning is probabilistic is a suggestion about moral logic, not about moral psychology. It is a suggestion about how people should reason, not about how they do reason. Discovering how people do perform moral reasoning is the task of social psychology, not moral philosophy. So long as people reason in accord with the calculus of probabilities, it does not matter whether they use the calculus of probabilities in their reasoning processes. Similarly, if people make inferences that are in accord with logical deductions, then it does not matter if they do not structure their reasoning in the rigorous way a mathematician would when proving a theorem. Logic tells people what conclusions they should come to based on their initial premises; it is not an account of how they do reason. Nor does logic tell people whether a premise is true or not, it only tells people what would follow from the premise if it were true. Similarly, probabilistic moral reasoning does not tell people the values that the conditional probabilities measuring the support given by reasons to conclusions should take; it only tells people how their degrees of confidence in their decisions should change in response to the reasons that they consider.

These conclusions may seem unhelpful. No one knows the exact conditional probabilities to assign to pieces of moral advice. Most people are bad at the explicit manipulation of probabilities, even if they know their values. For example, most university students find probability and statistics courses to be difficult. So even if the exact probabilities were known, most people would still find explicit, deliberative, and conscious moral reasoning overly difficult. By contrast, most people are quite good at the implicit manipulation of probabilities. As a species, human beings have evolved under conditions of uncertainty about food, safety, shelter, reproduction, and social interactions. Just as a gambler whose confidence levels did not correspond to the realities of the blackjack table would go bankrupt, a species with individuals whose implicit confidence levels were not able to adapt to the realities of life in an uncertain world would go extinct. Even though behavioral economists and social psychologists have discovered some biases in the way people unconsciously learn and manipulate probabilities, people are still quite good at intuiting how to combine probabilities.

So, we are led back to the advice of W.D. Ross about intuiting what to do: "This sense of our particular duty in particular circumstances, preceded and informed by the fullest reflection we can bestow on the act in all its bearings, is highly fallible, but it is the only guide we have to our duty" (Ross and Stratton-Lake 2002, 42). Our contemporary understanding of intuition is different from that of Ross. Ross thought that moral intuition was a mysterious faculty of the mind that could apprehend *prima facie* obligations and how to balance them. Modern psychology understands intuition to be the unconscious processing of information in an extremely fast manner by the brain. Intuition is not instinct; for humans, it is more like a skill that they can learn. For example, skilled mathematicians intuitively see how to solve problems that are beyond the skills of beginners. Mathematicians become skilled at problem-solving in part by taking advice (in the form of theorems) about what features of the problems to pay attention to and in part by practice with appropriate feedback. Similarly, moral agents can develop their skills at applying moral reasoning, in small part by taking the fallible advice of those who have thought deeply about similar problems, and in large part by practice in the context of the feedback generated by discussion and debate.

To apply ethical reasoning to a complicated case, all of us must learn to balance the sometimes-conflicting advice given by various ethical theories, where each theory calls attention to specific features of the situation. We can arrive at an overall decision by first thinking of the decision process as analogous to a boardroom situation where different theories each present their own viewpoint. Then, with the various reasons in mind, we can go on to weigh them, not on a metaphorical balance scale, but according to the plausibility of each reason and the likelihood that each reason confers on a specific conclusion about the best decision.

6.4 Exercises

1. (a) What is the highest value that a probability measure can take? (b) What is this value in percentage terms? (c) What is the maximum value that someone's degree of confidence can take in percentage terms? (d) What is the maximum weight that a physical object can have?
2. The shooter rolls a single, fair, six-sided die. (a) What is the probability of getting a three? (b) The shooter conceals the rolled die and announces truthfully that it is a number greater than, but not equal to, three. What is the conditional probability that it is a two, given that the number is greater than three? (c) What is the conditional probability that it is a four, given that the number is greater than three? (d) Consider the fact that the number showing is greater than three as a reason for a conclusion. Does it offer the same support to the conclusion that the number showing is a two as it does to the conclusion that the number showing is a four?
3. The Moral Machine is a website that asks people to consider possible scenarios that a self-driving car might face and to say what they would do in that scenario. Browse the website, <http://moralmachine.mit.edu/>, and participate in the research if so moved.

REFERENCES

Aristotle. 350 BCE. *Politics*. Translated by Benjamin Jowett, accessed December 28, 2010, <http://classics.mit.edu/Aristotle/politics.html>
Bentham, Jeremy. 1823. *Introduction to the Principles of Morals and Legislation*. 2nd ed, accessed November 16, 2010, <http://www.econlib.org/library/Bentham/bnthPML18.html>
Crane, Andrew, and Dirk Matten. 2004. *Business Ethics, a European Perspective: Managing Corporate Citizenship and Sustainability in the Age of Globalization*. Oxford and New York: Oxford University Press.
Dancy, Jonathan. 2004. *Ethics Without Principles*. Oxford: Clarendon Press.
Gilbert, Daniel. 2006. *Stumbling on Happiness*. New York: Alfred A. Knopf.
Gilligan, Carol. 1982. *In a Different Voice: Psychological Theory and Women's Development*. Cambridge: Harvard University Press.
Greene, Joshua. 2014. *Moral Tribes: Emotion, Reason, and the Gap Between Us and Them*. New York: Penguin.
Hume, David. 1740. *A Treatise of Human Nature*, accessed August 10, 2010, <http://www.gutenberg.org/ebooks/4705>
Kahneman, Daniel. 2011. *Thinking, Fast and Slow*. Toronto: Anchor.
Kant, Immanuel. 1959. *Foundations of the Metaphysics of Morals*. Translated by Lewis White Beck. Indianapolis: Bobbs Merrill.

Leopold, Aldo. 1970. *A Sand County Almanac*. New York: Ballantine.
Locke, John. 1689. *Second Treatise of Government*, accessed October 29, 2010, <http://www.gutenberg.org/ebooks/7370>
Mill, John Stuart. 1859. *On Liberty*, accessed May 27, 2013, <http://www.gutenberg.org/files/34901/34901-h/34901-h.htm>
Nozick, Robert. 1974. *Anarchy, State, and Utopia*. New York: Basic Books.
———. 1989. *The Examined Life*. New York: Simon and Shuster.
Rawls, John. 1971. *A Theory of Justice*. Cambridge: Harvard University Press.
Regan, Tom. 1983. *The Case for Animal Rights*. Berkeley: University of California Press.
Ross, W. D[avid]. 2002. *The Right and the Good*. Ed. Philip Stratton-Lake. Oxford: Clarendon Press.
Sandel, Michael. 2009. *Justice: What's the Right Thing to Do?* New York: Farrar, Straus and Giroux.
Singer, Peter. 1976. "All Animals Are Equal." In Peter Singer, ed., *Animal Rights and Human Obligations*. Englewood Cliffs, NJ: Prentice Hall.
Smart, J.J.C., and Bernard Williams. 1973. *Utilitarianism: For and Against*. Cambridge: Cambridge University Press.
Thomson, Judith Jarvis. 1976. "Killing, Letting Die, and the Trolley Problem." *The Monist* 59, 204–17.

INDEX

absolute duty, 49, 51–52
action-guiding aspect of ethical reasoning, 9
aggregate interests, 88–89
agreement-seeking aspect of ethical
    reasoning, 9, 11–12, 42, 51
animal ethics, 17
animal rights theories, 95
animal welfare, 60
animals, 36–37
    moral agency question, 17, 100
    moral standing, 116
anthropocentric theories, 113, 115
applied ethics, virtue in, 27
Aristotelians, 30
Aristotle, xi, 34, 36–37, 136
autonomous decision-making. *See under*
    moral autonomy

balancing care against justice, 40
balancing moral reasons, 125, 131–35
beneficence, 52
    prima facie duty of, 132
beneficence premise, 131
benevolence, 35
Bentham, Jeremy, xi, 72, 80, 82, 88, 136
    "Each to count for one, and none to count
        for more than one" (slogan), 87

An Introduction to the Principles of Morals
    and Legislation, 78
pleasure-maximizing principle, 35
Bentham's utilitarianism
    everyone's interests given equal
        importance, 78
business ethics, 17

capitalist market society. *See* free enterprise
    economic system
care ethics, 21, 26, 37–41
    approach to Transplant Case, 89
    care as mean between selfishness and self-
        sacrifice in, 40–41
    contrast with standard ethical theories, 39
    requires practical wisdom and sense of
        justice, 41
    responsibilities to others, 39
    social cooperation, 39
    special relationships in, 38–40
    virtues of care and wisdom, 39
    virtues of moral sensitivity and
        discernment, 39
categorical imperative, 50–51
causal responsibility, 97–98, 100–04, 106
    necessary condition, 101
    sufficient conditions, 102

character traits, 8, 19, 27, 37, 43
childhood moral training
   foundation for adult moral excellence, 31
children
   moral agency, 100
cognitively impaired persons, 58–59
combining moral reasons, 124–30
common good, 94
common good approach, 95
communitarian virtue ethic
   on moral standing, 115
communities
   Bentham's description, 88
   moral education by, 31, 42
   need to educate members in skills of critical thinking, 35
community-as-a-whole, 94
community-good approach
   compatible with extension of moral standing to ecosystems, 94
   free-ride problem, 95
community obligations, 35
compensatory justice, 101
conditional probability, 137–38
conflict of interest
   threat to autonomous decision-making 108–09
consequence-based theories, 17–18, 22–23, 55. *See also* utilitarianism
   assignment of moral standing, 116
   ethical egoism as, 74
   Footbridge Case, 130
   justification of moral rights, 56
   moral accountability in, 104
   Trolley Problem, 126
contractarian ethical theory, 76
contribution-based merit theories, 105
cooperation, 2, 30, 39, 41, 75
cooperation dilemma, 6
   potential contractarian solution to, 72
correlative duty, 48, 53–54, 57
cost-benefit analysis, 85–86, 89
creating moral value, 71–72
criminal law, 97–98
critical theory, 74
critical thinking, 35, 37
cross-cultural disagreements regarding ethical judgments, 14–15
cultural conservatism, 15, 34
cultural relativism, 14, 16, 34, 42–43

deception
   undermining moral autonomy, 108
decision-making by committee, 102
   moral accountability, 105
deontological theories, 21
derivative virtues, 27
difference principle, 66–67, 105
direct ethical obligations, 114–15
direct utilitarianism, 65, 90
discussion, wisdom, and judgment
   emphasized in care ethics, 21
distributive justice, 44, 49, 58–67, 74, 105
   expensive tastes problem, 65–66
   libertarianism approach to, 63–64
   utilitarian approach to, 64–65
Divine command theories of ethics, 48
Doctrine of the Double Effect, 129–30
dominant strategy in game theory, 5–6
duties, 21, 48–52. *See also* ethical obligations
   absolute duty, 49, 51–52
   correlative duty, 48, 53–54, 57
   prima facie duties, 48, 51–52, 131–32, 135–36
duties as basic principles, 48
duties as requirements of reason, 48
duty-based theories, 22
duty of justice, 52
duty of non-maleficence, 52
duty of self-improvement, 52

ecological ethical theories, 95
economic utilitarianism, 23, 84–88
   preference-satisfaction utilitarianism, 81–85
egoism and contractarianism, 74–77
emotional capacities, 2
emotional manipulation
   distinct from legitimate persuasion, 110
   threat to autonomous decision-making, 109–10
emotional reactions are action-guiding, 9
environmental ethics, 17
equal consideration of interests, 65
equality, moral, 60, 62
equality of opportunity, 62–63
equality of resources
   distributive justice, 65–66
equality of welfare, 65
ethical considerations
   conflicts with one another, 20, 122
ethical decision-making, 1, 8, 16, 19, 47

high-level skill, 121
ethical disagreement, 15
ethical duties from other people's moral rights. *See* correlative duty
ethical egoism, 23, 73–75, 77, 115
ethical intuition, 78, 140
ethical obligations, 11–12, 114–15
 of family membership, 33
 prima facie rather than absolute, 135
ethical pluralism, 120–24
ethical principles, 7–8, 48
ethical reasoning, 8, 19. *See also* moral reasoning
 action-guiding, 9
 agreement-seeking, 9, 12
 balance sometimes-conflicting advice of various theories, 140
ethical relativism, 13–16, 34, 74
ethical theories, 2, 18–21, 120
evaluating motivations of decision makers, 47
evil person, 17
evolutionary and molecular biology explanations, 94
expensive tastes problem, 65–66
experience-based utilitarianism, 78–80, 116
Experience Machine thought experiment, 79–80

failure to disclose information threat to autonomous decision-making, 108
fair equality of opportunity, 62–63
fairness, 79
feminism, 38
feminist ethics of care, 21. *See also* women
"First, do no harm," 90
flourishing, 27, 30
 in teleological consequentialism, 92
 as understood in virtue ethics, 29
 virtue ethics, 31–32, 93
Footbridge Case, 129
formal equality of opportunity, 62
free enterprise economic system, 37, 64
 market price for a commodity, 85
 market society, virtues of, 42
friendship, 75

game theory, 2
Gilligan, Carol, *In a Different Voice*, 37
good in non-moral sense confused with moral sense, 93

good life, 32
good reasoning alone not enough, 3
governments with power to punish cheating, 75

happiness, x, 23, 29, 55, 65, 72, 74, 139
 in experience-based utilitarianism, 79
 in indirect utilitarianism, 90
 in preference-satisfaction utilitarianism, 81, 83
Harm Principle, 35, 49, 55
Hippocratic Oath, 90
Hobbes, Thomas, 75
holistic form of consequentialism, 116
holistic theories, 92
holistic theories of moral value
 community-as-a-whole in, 94–96
holistic view of organizational moral accountability, 105
Homer, 34, 37, 42
honor killing, 14–15
human flourishing. *See* flourishing
human rights. *See under* rights
Hume, David, 10
Hume's Guillotine, 10
hypothetical imperative, 50

identity-based feminism, 38
identity-based reasoning, 104
identity-based theories, 18, 20–21
impartiality, 39
In a Different Voice (Gilligan), 37
indirect ethical obligations, 114–15
indirect utilitarianism, 74, 88–91, 106
individual causal responsibility, 103
individual moral accountability
 in committee decision-making, 105
informed preference theory of value, 83–84, 95
interest theory, 57
interest theory of moral rights, 58, 116
An Introduction to the Principles of Morals and Legislation (Bentham), 78
is-ought gap, 10–11, 78, 97

justice, 31, 35. *See also* distributive justice; retributive justice
justice, theories of, 22, 42, 59
justice and moral equality, 59–61
justice approach to Transplant Case, 89
justifying moral rights, 56–59

Kant, Immanuel, xi, 35, 48–51, 123, 136
    absolute ethical duties, 49
    categorical imperative, 22, 50–51
lawn-crossing problem, 90, 103
legal coercion, 75–76
legal duties, 48
legal ethics, 18
legal rights, 54
legal standing, 113
Leopold, Aldo, 94
    land ethic, 95
libertarianism, 105
    approach to distributive justice, 63–64
liberties
    impose duties on others, 49
liberty, 35
Locke, John, 35, 64

Mead, Margaret, 14
Mill, John Stuart, 35
    Harm Principle, 35, 55
    On Liberty, 55
moral accountability, 97, 101, 104–06
    identity-based reasoning, 104
    to those with moral standing, 115
    virtue ethics on, 98
moral accountability of organizations, 105–06
moral agency, 18, 57, 99–100
    children, 100
    wilderness areas, 17
moral agent, 17, 99–100, 138–39
moral autonomy, 35, 57, 63, 84, 106–10
    autonomous decision making, 108–09
    capacity for autonomous choice, 57
    coercive threat to, 108
    lying or deception as threat to, 108
moral competence, 28, 136
moral deliberation, 136
moral dilemma, 129
moral emotions, 77
moral intuition, 140
moral perception, 28, 38
moral reasoning, 39, 134. *See also* ethical reasoning
    analogy to scientific reasoning, 137
    balancing probabilities, 136
    fallible moral reasoning, 135–41
    probabilistic, 139–40

moral responsibility, 98
moral rights, 53, 55–59
moral rights, extension to the non-human world, 57
moral rights of another person, 48, 53–55.
    See also correlative duty
moral standing, 19, 112–17
    entities that have natural purpose, 93
    ethics of care on, 115
    holistic theories of, 114
    individualistic theories of, 114
    infant humans, 116
    nonhuman entities: animals, plants, ecosystems, 94, 113
moral value, 16, 72, 92
morally relevant differences between people, 60
motivation-based reasoning, 104
motivation by ethical principles, 48

natural rights, 56–58
natural rights to self-ownership, 63
naturalistic fallacy, 10
necessary and sufficient cause, 128
necessary condition, 101–03
negative moral right, 55
negative right, 54, 128
negative rights of self-ownership, 63–64, 130
non-anthropocentric ethical views, 113
non-derivative justification for moral rights, 56
non-psychological consequentialism, 22
non-psychological consequentialist theories, 116
non-psychological moral value, 92
normative cost-benefit analysis, 85–87
normative economics, 85
normative force of a moral reason, 134
Nozick, Robert, 79–80

objective consequentialism, 83
objective happiness, 29
On Liberty (Mill), 55
organization, corporation, or governmental department
    moral agency, 17, 99–100
organizational moral accountability
    holistic view of, 105
    under indirect utilitarianism, 106
ought-implies-can principle, 11–12, 89

paradox of egoism, 75
payoff matrix, 4
personal autonomy, 107
pleasure-maximizing principle, 35
political philosophy, 59
positive economics, 85
positive right, 54, 128
practical wisdom, 28, 41
prediction, 100
preference-based utilitarianism, 81, 116
preference intensities, 87
preference-satisfaction utilitarianism, 81–85
prima facie duties, 48, 51–52, 135–36
   conflicts between, 131–32
prima facie duty of beneficence, 132
prima facie ethical obligations, 135
principle, 19
principle-based theories, 18–19, 21–22
Prisoner's Dilemma Game, 2–3, 6, 30, 41, 43, 72, 76
privacy rights, 58–59
private property rights, 63–64
probabilistic moral generalities, 136
probabilistic version of the duty of fidelity, 136
probability, 138
probability as a guide to life, 139
prosocial emotions, 3, 7–8, 33
prosocial virtues, 34
psychological consequentialism or utilitarianism, 22
psychological egoism, 74–77
psychological moral value, 92

racism, 60
rational agents, 23
rational moral agent, 138–39
Rawls, John
   difference principle, 105
   A Theory of Justice, 66
reason, virtue of, 34
reasoning abilities, 2
reasoning in an ethically pluralist framework, 125
retributive justice, 97–98, 101
reward and punishment, 42, 44
   distributed differently in different cultures, 43
   proportionality in, 43–44
   role in educating people in virtue, 42
right to privacy, 58–59

rights, 35, 56–59, 116
   general right, 53
   human rights, 56, 74
   moral (*See* moral rights)
   natural rights, 56–58, 63
   negative rights, 54–55, 63–64, 128, 130
   positive rights, 54, 128
   private property rights, 63–64
   specific rights, 53
   will-based rights, 58–59
   will theory of rights, 57, 115
rights-based approach, 55, 106, 128
rights-based theories, 22
rights of individuals, 35, 90
Roman Catholic jurisprudence, 129
Ross, W.D., 132, 135–36, 140
   prima facie duties, 52, 131
rules
   acceptance of, 76
   internalization, 77
   obedience to, 90

saintly altruism, 73–74
self-interest, 30, 74, 77
self-ownership, 63–64, 77
self-punishment, 77
self-regarding reasons, 104
sensitivity to needs of others, 38
sexism, 60
Singer, Peter
   on animal welfare, 61
   on speciesism, 60
skills, traits, or dispositions, 27
slaves, 36–37, 61
social conditions
   flourishing from, 30
social cooperation, 2, 27, 31–32, 39, 41
special relationships, 38–40
speciesism, 60
specific obligations, 32
specific right, 53
Stoics, 30
subjective happiness, 29
sufficient condition, 101–02

teleological and holistic ethics, 91–96
teleological approach to moral value, 93
teleological conceptual framework, 92
teleological consequentialism, 116
   flourishing in, 92

moral agent in, 92
A Theory of Justice (Rawls), 66
thought experiments, 79, 120. See also names for specific thought experiments
Transplant Case, 56, 89–90
    rights of victim outweigh utilitarian consideration, 123
    utilitarian intuition on, 123
Trolley Problem, 125–30
    moral dilemma, 129
Truth-teller and the Axe-murderer, 52
    Kant's Categorical Imperative and, 51
    maximizing utility outweighs right to hear truth, 124
    utilitarian intuitions on, 123

Ultimatum Game, 3, 6–7
unintended consequences, 125–26
universalizability, 51–52
    ethical judgments, 11
utilitarian intuitions, 123
utilitarian moral law, 123
utilitarianism, 22–23, 35, 62, 64–65, 72–73, 78
    on Truth-teller and the Axe-Murderer, 51
utilitarianism as decision-making technique, 89–90
utility, 72–73

vices, 20, 27
virtue, 20, 28
    as mean between two vices, 28–29, 40
virtue approach to Transplant Case, 89
virtue ethics, 20–21, 26–30
    character traits as guides (criticism), 35
    charge of cultural relativism, 34
    communitarian background, 35
    flourishing, 31–32, 93
    foundational assumptions, 31
    just system of reward and punishment in, 42

moral accountability, 104
moral agent in, 93
    on moral standing, 115
    organizations can have non-mental dispositions, 105–06
    problem of multiple community memberships, 36
    virtue ethics rule of action
    emulate the actions of a virtuous person, 28, 35
virtues, 27
    enable cooperation, 33–34
    forms of moral excellence, 27
    permanent character traits, 30–31
    prosocial character traits, 33
    skills in making ethical decisions, 31
virtues and vices relative to community standards, 34, 36, 42–43
virtues inculcated by community, 32
virtues of care and wisdom, 39
virtues of moral sensitivity and discernment, 39
virtues of rationality and wisdom, 37
virtues required by persons with different roles in society, 33
virtuous communities, 33
virtuous people, 28, 35
    can predict one another's behavior, 31
    obligations through membership in community, 32–33

weighing metaphor, 132–33, 135
White, David, xi
will-based rights, 58–59
will theory of rights, 57, 115
willingness-to-pay, 84, 86–87
wisdom, virtue of, 28, 34
wisdom and virtue, 33–37
women, 36–37, 61. See also feminist ethics of care

FROM THE PUBLISHER

A NAME NEVER SAYS IT ALL, BUT THE WORD "BROADVIEW" expresses a good deal of the philosophy behind our company. We are open to a broad range of academic approaches and political viewpoints. We pay attention to the broad impact book publishing and book printing has in the wider world; for some years now we have used 100% recycled paper for most titles. Our publishing program is internationally oriented and broad-ranging. Our individual titles often appeal to a broad readership too; many are of interest as much to general readers as to academics and students.

Founded in 1985, Broadview remains a fully independent company owned by its shareholders—not an imprint or subsidiary of a larger multinational.

For the most accurate information on our books (including information on pricing, editions, and formats) please visit our website at www.broadviewpress.com. Our print books and ebooks are also available for sale on our site.

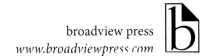

This book is made of paper from well-managed FSC® - certified forests, recycled materials, and other controlled sources.